The Book of Golf Disasters

Peter Dobereiner

Illustrations by John Ireland

PERENNIAL LIBRARY

Harper & Row, Publishers
New York, Cambridge, Philadelphia, San Francisco
London, Mexico City, São Paulo, Singapore, Sydney

THE BOOK OF GOLF DISASTERS. Text Copyright © 1983 by Peter Dobereiner. Illustrations copyright © 1983 by Hutchinson Publishing Group. All rights reserved. Printed in the United States of America. No part of this book may be used or reproduced in any manner whatsoever without written permission except in the case of brief quotations embodied in critical articles and reviews. For information address Atheneum Publishers, 115 Fifth Avenue, New York, NY 10003. Published simultaneously in Canada by Fitzhenry & Whiteside Limited, Toronto.

First PERENNIAL LIBRARY edition published 1986.

Library of Congress Cataloging-in-Publication Data

Dobereiner, Peter.
    The book of golf disasters.

    1. Golf—Anecdotes, facetiae, satire, etc.   I. Title.
GV967.D59 1986   796.352′0207   85-45187
ISBN 0-06-097017-0 (pbk.)

89 90 MPC 10

The Book of Golf Disasters

BOOKS BY PETER DOBEREINER

For Rachel

Contents

Introduction

Let us get one thing straight right from the start. This book is unashamedly peppered with words like disaster, tragedy and crisis. From long experience I know that the use of such terms is deeply offensive to a certain type of narrow-minded, self-important idiot with an excessively literal view of the world. 'How can you describe the missing of a three-foot putt as a disaster when millions of children are starving in Asia? After all, golf is only a game. You are devaluing the currency of the English language.' And so on *ad infinitum*, not to mention *nauseam*.

By way of a counterpunch to such assaults, I enlist the support of that windy penny-a-liner, William Shakespeare. He was dreadfully prolix and hadn't the slightest idea how to devise a decent plot but even after all these years he still has a good reputation in the business. He knew how to handle words. And he did not hestitate to describe *King Lear* as a tragedy. What is so tragic about actors being overpaid to do something they thoroughly enjoy?

Sport is just as much make-believe as drama. It is conducted within the framework of an invented reality which is quite different from the reality of life. It has its own laws and its own morality and its own conventions and its own scale of emotions. Within that artificial context the word disaster may be entirely appropriate to the missing of a short putt.

Besides, golf for professional golfers is not 'only' a game. It is a career, and disaster in the make-believe world of sport may also prove to be a personal disaster in the real world of life. So I make no apology for using terms which, in other circumstances, might be more appropriate to famine, plague and the loss of the *Titanic*. For these reasons I have omitted from this book any 'real' disasters, such as the car crash which so nearly ended Ben Hogan's life. Time did not throw a humorous light on that episode and that has been my criterion in selecting incidents; I have tried to find moments of excruciating embarrassment or disappointment whose recollection brings at least a wry smile to the victims in retrospect. That is really the whole joke because, while emotions on the golf course are all too real at the time, we can look back and see them in the perspective of the make-believe world of sport and laugh at our extravagant reactions.

The material for this book has been gathered from many sources, most of it at first hand from conversations with the victims. It is surprising how quickly you become hardened to the misfortune of other people. During the first few interviews I felt the odd pang or two of sympathy although, as a very bad player, I was never in much of a mood to burst into tears when a golfer recounted how his three-wood shot over the water failed by a foot to make the 287-yard carry, and he lost by a stroke, having to settle for a paltry $30,000 second prize.

But as the work proceeded I became almost inured to disaster, rather in the way a casualty surgeon becomes immune to the shock of the daily parade of mangled bodies. I found myself becoming as impatient as a drug addict, avid for ever more horrors. 'Yes, yes, go on. What happened after the mad dog bit off your index finger? Did you break a leg and score 120?' It was therefore a surprise to discover that my emotions were still capable of normal responses, and the man whose story penetrated my case-hardened defences was Joe Di Maggio. 'Golf disaster? Golf provided the greatest disaster of my life.'

In case an alien from some distant galaxy should chance upon this book I should add that Joe Di Maggio was a baseball player of quite exceptional talent and presence, equivalent perhaps in prowess and public affection to Arnold Palmer in golf. The converse also holds, for as a golfer Di Maggio equates with Palmer as a baseball player, with high marks for enthusiasm and the less said about performance the better.

Tell me, please, about your golf disaster, Mr Di Maggio.

'Olympic Club, San Francisco, 1966,' he said, and a distant bell began to ring. 'I was following Palmer on the last day and he played sublimely for nine holes to open up a seven-stroke lead over Bill Casper.'

Of course, the big collapse, perhaps the most notorious disaster in golf history. But what had it to do with Joe Di Maggio?

'Well, like everyone else in Arnie's army I bled inside when he started to drop the odd shot and Casper picked up his birdies, but I wasn't really worried for Arnold. He still had a few shots in hand and, being Arnold, I knew he would kill the par-five and make the championship safe. I went ahead at the 16th and I was standing behind the ropes right where he hooked his drive into the rough. He was as close as that. When he left his three-iron in the rough I couldn't bear to watch any more. Besides, my eyes were full of tears. I never felt so awful and I just had to turn away.'

As everyone knows, Palmer's seven-stroke lead evaporated and he lost the play-off, but what struck me about the story was that Di Maggio should have picked it out as *his* disaster. The golfer is a selfish animal and a disaster is something which happens to him; if it happens to an opponent then that's golf, so dry your eyes and get on with the game. Di Maggio must have suffered innumerable disasters on the golf course over the years and yet the example he chose was someone else's. I always knew that he was an exceptional man and this incident reinforced that opinion.

Fortunately, golfers are an egocentric breed and when they are on the course a three-foot putt looms as the most important event not just in their lives but in the entire history of the universe. That is what makes golf the finest pastime devised by man, its capacity to absorb its adherents so intensely that for the time being it is all of life.

Chi Chi Rodriguez defines golf as the most fun you can have without taking off your clothes. Yes, but it does not always work out that way. This book is a celebration of the coitus interruptus of the game, of the worst experiences you can have without taking off your clothes.

My sincere thanks go to all those golfers who have cooperated by reviving their most painful memories on the course. By way of consolation I offer the thought that this book has no pretensions to being the definitive history of golf disasters. The game has been played for at least 500 years and that fact makes it virtually impossible for any golfer to claim that his experience was the worst-ever disaster, or come to that, the best-ever performance. There is comfort in the reflection that someone, somewhere, at some time had a worse catastrophe.

1

Defeat snatched from the very jaws of victory

For all sad words of tongue and pen,
the saddest are these: 'It might have been!'

John Greenleaf Whittier

Will evil flow from the bottle?
Yes, a lot'll

Start a discussion of disasters in any golf club and you can be sure that someone will bring up Bradshaw's bottle. In order to savour the horrors of this incident to the full it may be helpful if I first say a word or two about the man for whom the fates had planned a doleful destiny in the Open Championship of 1949 at Royal St George's, Sandwich.

Harry Bradshaw is probably the only professional golfer in history who learnt his trade from the Bible. As an adolescent Bradshaw was befriended by an elderly priest, Father Gleeson, who detected a rich talent in the stocky youth. The priest guided the moral and spiritual development of Harry and each evening they would go to the practice hole at Delgany bearing clubs, balls, a folding chair and enlightening literature.

Their usual practice was to select a spot about a hundred yards from the hole. 'Now, Harry, you will hit approach shots and we will not leave this spot until you have holed one.' So saying, the priest would settle down on his folding chair and absorb himself in devotional reading. Both gave full attention to their duties, the one with his missal and the other with his missiles.

We can well imagine the free-spirited Irish lad suffering agonies of frustration, self-doubt and despair during these sessions. At these times the priest gave Harry strength to continue by encouraging him with an enlightening parable or an elevating illustration from the scriptures.

As a result of this stern apprenticeship Harry Bradshaw grew up with a sense of values which had everything to do with moral rectitude and brotherly love and very little to do with personal glory and storing up riches on earth. He also acquired a short game of such virtuosity that, unless you knew his background, you might suspect that he had made a compact with the Devil.

Bradshaw was a considerable golfer, good enough to win the World Cup for Ireland in partnership with Christy O'Connor in the days when every nation sent its strongest team. At the time that Billy Casper was the best player in the world he was matched to play Bradshaw at Portmarnock. Dublin's book-makers, as shrewd a body of men as you will find outside the horse-trading industry, recognized that Bradshaw was past his prime and offered odds of 7 to 1 against the local man. The Portmarnock members were torn in their loyalties. On the one hand they felt that it would be a gross betrayal of friendship to back Casper, but at the same time here was an unrivalled opportunity to reverse the natural order of things and skin the bookies. They took their dilemma to Bradshaw. Typically, he granted them full dispensation to place their bets as they pleased with never a hint of embarrassment or guilt. 'Mind you,' added Bradshaw in a throw-away aside, 'Casper would beat me any-where else, and probably easily enough, but at Portmarnock? If anyone fancies a bet on me I won't disappoint them.' A nod is as good as a wink to a man with his pencil poised over a betting slip. Bradshaw's intimate knowledge of every swale and hum-mock on the links, combined with his sorcerer's touch on the wedge and putter, carried him to victory and there was plenty of extra cash in the pockets of the members to fund the celebration.

In that 1949 Open at Sandwich Bradshaw went out of bounds at the Suez Canal 14th but, despite that double-bogey, he led the first round with a 68. The cheery Irishman with his flat cap pulled over his nose resembled a ploughman rather than an athlete but he had demonstrated the deceptiveness of appear-ances often enough and a good crowd followed his progress in the second round. At the fifth hole he cut his drive into the rough and when he reached the spot he found his ball nestling in the bottom half of a broken beer bottle.

It crossed his mind at the time that there was some kind of molly-coddling rule, framed for the benefit of effete golfers who took themselves and their golf too seriously, to cover this situa-tion. But that would entail inconveniencing his playing com-panions and holding up those behind as he sent back to the

clubhouse for one of the gentlemen who organized the championship. It would be a long walk for the gentleman and, anyway, he might be busy. Besides, the idea of seeking help from the rule book offended Harry's notions of golf and of life. For a man nourished on the example of Daniel in the lion's den, a broken bottle seemed a trifling obstacle. Harry reached for his wedge like Solomon taking up the jawbone of an ass and, closing his eyes as a protection against flying glass, smote the foe with all his might.

From the resulting explosion and flying shrapnel the ball advanced about 25 yards and Bradshaw emerged with his composure shattered. He missed the green with his next shot and took six. He finished with a 77, one more than Bobby Locke, and tied at the halfway stage with the South African. They matched scores for the next two rounds, 68, 70, and so had to play off for the title. Locke won by the runaway margin of 12 strokes.

There is no doubt that the experience with the bottle and its effect on Bradshaw's equanimity for the rest of that second round cost him the championship. Years later I asked him how many hours of sleep he had lost reproaching himself for that fateful decision to play the ball as it lay.

'Never one single second, sir,' he answered cheerily. 'Of course, if I had sent for a ruling I might have won the championship but it would not have been right. Locke was the better player. He deserved to win.' That reaction was, for me, the most extraordinary sequel to an experience which might well have soured another player for life. For Harry Bradshaw, a man who has never entertained a malicious thought in his life, that famous disaster was not a disaster at all. It was a kind of justice.

By coincidence another of golf's blithe spirits had a similar experience. Freddie Tait, the exuberant Scottish amateur whose brilliant golf career was tragically curtailed by his death on active service with the Black Watch in the Boer War, found his ball in the depths of a condensed milk can. Tait at least was under no threat from flying glass and he pitched the can with his niblick onto the green. On landing the ball obligingly rolled clear and finished right by the hole.

Why artists occasionally cut off their ears

Spectators at most sporting events are interested primarily in the result of the contest. Winning and losing are, after all, the central issues and therefore the prime interest. The fans may be absorbed in tactical analysis and appreciation of technique but all such considerations are related to the final result.

Golf tournaments are different. The winning of a golf tournament does not normally loom as the paramount issue until the last few holes. Of course, every stroke of the 72 holes bears on the outcome but in the first three rounds or so play appears more as a winnowing process to determine who will not win. The emergence of an actual winner seems too remote and uncertain to engage the spectator's full attention. So, in those early stages, golf tournaments more resembled exhibitions than contests. The fans can wander from exhibit to exhibit and it is a measure of the richness of the game that they attend in their thousands for what might be likened to a window-shopping expedition. Some follow their individual favourites, some go with big names, some are drawn to watch the notable big hitters, while purists seek out the classical swings of Gene Littler and Sam Snead. And then there are the connoisseurs who like nothing better than to observe and marvel at the stroke-makers.

Today I suppose, it is necessary to explain what a stroke-maker is. The modern professional game has developed and refined the standard stroke to an astonishing degree, the theory being that if you hit the ball straight for the correct distance then there is no necessity for fancy swinging and spinning of the ball. Of course, every professional worth his corn can move the ball sideways through the air but this facility is kept as a last resort, to get past an inconvenient tree and suchlike.

The stroke-makers, and they are sadly a diminishing band, perceived golf as an art rather than an exercise in spatial geometry. They summed up the topography, air conditions, lie of the ball, ground consistency, the strategic implications and distance and then visualized the precise form of shot best suited to these factors. Every stroke was tailor-made for the occasion, fashioned to suit the unique situation. It may be a denigratory over-simplification to say that the modern pro reads 140 yards off his chart and responds automatically with a full wedge shot. But these days an average three-ball in a tournament would be likely to play much the same shot from this range. With the stroke-makers it was impossible to guess how each player would approach the problem. John Panton would as likely have cut a three-iron with a delicate stroke contrived of instinct and feel. Max Faulkner might have hit a wedge shot with full power which never rose above shoulder height, pitching short of the flag and stopping abruptly as if by magic close to the hole. Phil Rodgers had an astonishing repertory of approach shots and we can visualize him throwing the ball high into the air so it plummeted almost vertically to the flag. The hands were everything and when these craftsmen had the touch their golf was wondrous to behold.

Nobody had better hands than Tommy Bolt. He played with imagination and flair and manipulated the ball round a golf course by legerdemain. His contemporaries were often surprised by the sheer effrontery of the shots he attempted and then doubly surprised by the virtuosity with which he pulled them off. When he was good he was unbeatable and it seemed to be such an occasion in the Virginia Beach Open of 1954 when he opened with scores of 64, 62 to lead by seven strokes.

The third round was not good for Bolt and coming to the last hole his lead was down to one stroke, with Pete Cooper pressing him hard. The 18th of the Cavalier Country Club course is a par three of about 165 yards, over water. The sensible shot in the circumstances was to play for the fat of the green, for a safe three and a possible long putt for a two. The flag was sited at the edge of the green, hard by the water.

Nature is a bitch. Nature is never content to be generous and let it go at that. Nature always attaches strings to its gifts. Nature has to compensate. So, when nature endows someone with a massive artistic talent she balances the account by throwing in a massive artistic temperament. Thus it was in the case of Tommy Bolt. His artistic temperament scorned the safety-first policy of playing for the middle of the green. There could only be one way for Bolt, to pitch his ball to the flag. The stroke itself was, as usual, masterly. His club selection, however, left something to be desired. Precisely what it was that it left to be desired was a yard or so of carry. Splash! He made five and lost the tournament by one stroke.

Bolt ran to his car and did not remove his spiked shoes until he reached Baltusrol, site of the next tournament, the US Open. It is a pity that golf remembers Bolt more for his outbursts of temperament than for his stroke-making. Virginia Beach? Sure, that was when Thunderbolt drove out of the parking lot like a rocket still wearing his spikes. We might also remember that it was also when one of the game's great stroke-makers played 36 holes in 126 strokes, all different and all brilliant examples of a dying art.

Warning: road liable to severe depressions

The 17th hole of the Old Course at St Andrews, the notorious Road Hole, has broken many hearts and could provide its own book of disasters. One act of infamy must suffice.

David Ayton was a St Andrews man, a gifted player and the hero of the hour as he stepped onto the 17th tee in the final round (36 holes in those days) of the 1885 Open Championship five strokes clear of the field. He hit a good drive and a spanking brassie shot into prime position for a chip-and-run up the green to the flag.

With strokes aplenty in hand there was no call for heroics. Ayton could well afford a chip and two putts. He chipped gently, a fraction *too* gently. The ball just failed to hold its line on the cross-slope and rolled away, finishing in front of the bunker. He now had to pitch over the bunker and stop his ball on the narrow shelf of the green, with the treacherous road waiting beyond to punish a heavy-handed shot. It is a moot point whether a ball in this position is the most terrifying shot in the entire world of golf, given the circumstances of the Open Championship trophy waiting to be claimed in a matter of minutes. Some advanced students of sadism claim that in those days before the introduction of the broad-soled wedge the torture might have been fractionally more acute if the ball had been in the bunker.

Anyway, Ayton's pitch failed to hold the green and rolled down onto the road. He tried to scuttle the ball on the bank and it rolled back onto the road. Too gentle, too strong, too gentle . . . now he was too strong again, putting the ball into the bunker.

He failed to get out of the sand with his first attempt. Now, with dry mouth and pumping heart, he tried again. Still the mocking ball remained in the sand. That was his last chance. Now it was too late. He got the ball out with his third attempt, two-putted for an 11 and lost the Open by two strokes.

The day that the wisecracks dried up

Every competitor in a major tournament is, by definition, a highly accomplished striker of the golf ball. Luck is often a factor, although mostly a minor one, and what really determines the outcome are human qualities of nerve, character and experience. These are just some of the elements that make up a winning temperament and in no golfer are they more starkly epitomized than the redoubtable Lee Trevino. If you had to nominate a professional golfer to play for your life in a tight finish you could not do better than select the battling Mexican-American. After all, Trevino learnt his trade by playing for his own life, earning the groceries in the toughest of all games – the $10 Nassau when you have only a quarter in your pocket. Yes, he must be the man to play for your life.

Had your fate depended on Trevino's golf in the 1969 Alcan Golfer of the Year tournament at Portland, Oregon, you would have spent most of the week in a rising tide of optimism. After 69 holes you would have been justified in throwing your cap in the air and shouting 'I'm saved. The signing of the reprieve is just a formality.' *Requiescat in pace*, friend.

Trevino was in typically ebullient mood that week. He opened with rounds of 70, 67, 69 to lead Billy Casper, his only serious rival, by two strokes. On the last day Casper, playing in front, was steady but unspectacular, just about keeping ahead of par. Trevino, on the other hand, was inspired. He had five birdies in the space of six holes through the turn and then repaired the damage of a dropped stroke with another birdie and an eagle. By the slightly uncertain measure of their relative standings against par, Trevino was ahead by a street with four holes to play: Trevino −17, Casper −10. In the press room the golf correspondents with tight deadlines were hammering out their account of Trevino's triumph. *Mea culpa*.

There was no cause to rip those reports from our typewriters when Casper holed a long birdie putt at the 15th, nor when he followed suit at the 16th, nor even when Trevino pulled his drive at the 16th behind a tree and the stymie cost him a stroke. He still had four strokes in hand, the players were running out of opportunities for either triumph or disaster and all would surely be well. The copy might require a slight muting of the more extravagant adjectives but the central narrative of a Trevino victory would stand.

At the short 17th Trevino strayed from the habit of a lifetime. His normal routine is to insist that his caddie tells him the precise yardage to his target and add such pertinent information as the wind strength and direction, the state of the ground and the proximity of hazards. Nothing more. Trevino wants an assessment of the problem but no hint of a suggestion as to the club or type of shot. That is the golfer's business, especially in the case of a highly individual player like Trevino. He is the only one who can make the vital judgements about how he perceives the shot, how he feels and how he wants to fashion the stroke.

On this occasion the caddie proffered the nine-iron and, despite faint misgivings, Trevino took it. For once he was not totally clear in his mind about the shot he wanted to hit and this grain of indecision got into the works. The ball fell short into a bunker. Trevino cursed himself for his lapse and failed to recover at his first attempt. The second sand shot was well below the usual Trevino standard, on the green but a long way from the hole. He took three putts at about the time that Casper was rolling in his fourth successive birdie putt on the 18th green.

Casper, who had been concentrating his ambitions on securing second place, was astonished to see the scoreboard change. He was in at 14 under par and there was Trevino at 13 under with one to play.

Trevino was not cracking any jokes as he played the last, and he played it well. He hit his approach to 15 feet but the birdie putt he needed to force the play-off stayed out. Casper's winning spoils amounted to $55,000, Trevino collected $15,000 for his second place. Casper worked out that those four birdie putts on the last four holes had netted him $1000 a foot.

We writers had to do the fastest rewrite job of our lives.

The inferno in a straw hat

It is a moot point whether Sam Snead or Roberto de Vicenzo won more tournaments than anyone else in the history of golf. It all depends on how you define a tournament and, in any case, it does not really matter. Snead's credentials as one of the greatest players of all time would be impressive enough with half his achievements. It is therefore a pity that whenever his career comes up for discussion it is inevitable that someone will remark that his record is incomplete because he never won his own national championship. From here it is a short step for an intellectual 24-handicapper to launch into a dissertation on the theme that Snead was the supreme journeyman but not quite in the master craftsman class of the true champions, implying that some unspecified character defect prevented him from winning the US Open. Snead has thus gone into mythology of golf unfairly labelled 'the man who never won the Open'. That is rather like dismissing the military genius of Napoleon by branding him 'the man who could not beat Wellington'.

Snead's Waterloo came early in his career at the 1939 US Open at Spring Mill, Philadelphia. I have no doubt at all that if the Open had been held under the smooth organization of the modern United States Golf Association then Snead would have breezed it. In those days tournaments were informal, even haphazard affairs. Everyone went out· to play and at the end of the day they added up the scores to determine the winner. Lack of information and lack of organization defeated Snead that day.

He knew that par figures on the last two holes would give him a total of 281 which would equal the Open record and therefore surely be good enough to win. He was strong with his approach to the 71st green and made a bogey. Well, that might not be too desperate. Or was it? He had half an hour to brood on his prospects before the last tee was clear.

By this time Byron Nelson was in with a total of 284 and no one on the course was in a position to threaten that score. It sounds extraordinary in these days of computerized scoring systems and instantaneous leader boards but nobody thought to tell Snead the position, that he could win with a six on the last hole. Instead of playing the last hole safely, Snead in his ignorance thought he had to gamble on a birdie and he went for a long drive. The ball finished in the rough which had been trampled down by spectators and the lie, although sandy, was good enough to persuade Snead that he could make the green with his brassie.

The clubface contacted high on the ball which flew low about 160 yards into a fairway bunker, partially burying in the fluffy sand. He felt that he had to hit the green 110 yards away and so he selected his eight-iron. It was a high-risk shot and the gamble failed by a fraction, the ball plugging in a crevice between fresh turfs which had been laid along the lip.

Now he had to play a hit-and-hope shot, blasting into the turf with all his strength. The ball shot left into another bunker 40 yards away.

It was at this point that a spectator told Snead that he had two strokes left to equal the 284 of Nelson. He was furious and felt, with good reason as it transpired, that he had been the victim of a conspiracy of silence which had pushed him into a rash strategy. To his credit he contrived a good bunker shot from a bad lie, having to stand outside the bunker and crouch to the ball, and his 40-foot putt caught the side of the cup and rolled three feet away. Snead's world collapsed and in his black mood of anger and frustration he missed the next putt, for the most notorious eight in American golf. That one hole haunted him for the rest of his life.

Counting Arnold's chickens

When I asked Arnold Palmer to probe beneath the scar tissue of his psyche and relate the worst disaster of his adventurous career, I was merely seeking confirmation that it would involve the 1966 US Open at the Olympic Club of San Francisco when he lost a seven-stroke lead in the last nine holes, and the championship itself.

But no, from a rich treasury of well-publicized disasters he debated between two self-inflicted wounds with the seven-iron. There was the seven-iron shot which got him into triple-bogey trouble on the 70th hole of the 1982 Vintage Invitational seniors tournament and cost him first place. This was a recent and therefore painful memory, but on balance he plumped for the deeper wound of the 1961 Masters.

As he stood on the 72nd tee he was one hole away from his third Masters victory in four years and the first successful defence of the title in the history of the championship. The euphoria in the gallery can be imagined as the most popular golfer of all time, playing in front of his adoring army, hitched his pants, wrapped his massive hands around the grip of his driver and whaled into the shot with that characteristic and aggressive twiddle on the follow-through. The ball flew like a shell straight and true up the fairway, a colossal drive into the steep upslope of about 260 yards. The army exploded in delight. Arnie was on a charge. Gary Player was in the clubhouse with a score of 280 and Palmer needed a par to win. After that drive the rest, surely, was a formality.

The 18th green of Augusta National is generously large and tilted invitingly to receive the approach shot. At a range of 150 yards it was perfect for Palmer's seven-iron.

As he walked up the fairway with the tumult ringing in his ears and friends slapping his back in anticipatory congratulations, Palmer unconsciously fell victim to over-confidence. The fastest way to lose concentration on the golf course is through being over-confident and without concentration even the greatest player is done for.

In anticipation of the vision of his ball smacking into the turf of the green, Palmer came off the shot ever so slightly. It was not a bad shot but he did not quite get all the ball on the meat of the clubface and this fractional imprecision was just enough to make the ball tail off in the air and drop into the right-hand bunker. The shot jolted Palmer but his position was by no means critical. 'All I had to do was splash out of the bunker, leaving me a putt for victory or two putts for a play-off with Player.'

All I had to do. . . . The very phrase is a temptation to the fates and the ruination of concentration. Of course it *was* an easy shot for a bunker player of Palmer's ability but even for the best player shots are only easy if they are given the fullest attention. In other words they are easy in retrospect but never a foregone conclusion. Palmer's second mistake was in thinking that he had only to splash the ball out to the hole. After all his emotions had raced ahead of events and he was already being invested in his green jacket. He was, as he later recognized, rather hasty in playing his recovery shot and again he caught the ball thin. The clubhead needed to cut into the sand a little earlier and a little deeper. Instead of the classic explosion the ball came out as if played for a forcing bunker shot and it went across the green, running down the far slope.

Palmer is the author of that wise advice concerning short shots to the green: your worst chip will finish as close as your best pitch, and your worst putt will finish as close as your best chip. He took the putter and ran the ball 15 feet past the cup. Now he needed to hole the return for a tie with Player. The ball touched the rim of the hole and stayed out. Palmer finished in a tie for second place.

God must be a Mexican

There are plenty of professionals who win tournaments with splendid golf but who cannot reproduce that form in the major championships. Then there is a small minority who cannot do themselves justice in the routine circuit events but who rise to the occasion for the majors. Jack Nicklaus is the most obvious example and I make no apology for mentioning Tony Jacklin in the same breath.

Once he had won the British and American Open Championships Jacklin could not get inspired by lesser events. Ten years after those triumphs it is probably true to say that he played tournaments for fun and really competed at full throttle for one week in a year, in the Open Championship. That is not to say that he did not try. Fun for Jacklin, as with Nicklaus, means competition, and both throw themselves into the fray with relish. They want to give of their best but it does not happen. Without the tension and excitement which surrounds a major championship, the adrenalin does not flow to the point where they become elevated into a different plane and achieve their full golfing potential.

In the case of Jacklin this rarefied state of mind is a condition of extreme delicacy, vulnerable to rupture by external pressures. In my judgement he is unlucky not to have won the British Open Championship four times. At St Andrews he achieved that magical state of golfing grace in which the club swings itself and the player can concentrate his mind entirely on selecting his targets and visualizing the trajectory of the shot he needs to hit.

Jacklin played sublime golf to be out in 29 when a cloudburst halted play for the day and completely destroyed his mood. The same thing happened at Lytham when he was penalized for what he had intended as an act of sportsmanship of which more later. But Muirfield in 1972 was the disaster which scarred him for life and very possibly altered the course of his career.

At the halfway stage Jacklin was tied in the lead with the defending champion, Lee Trevino, and they were paired together for the fateful third round. Jacklin pulled clear of his rival and he began to see Nicklaus in terms of his main challenger, not that Jack was doing anything spectacular, but he was keeping within striking distance and every professional golfer gets an uneasy feeling whenever Nicklaus is in the offing.

Then, so far as Jacklin was concerned, the most insidious disasters of his career began. On the 14th green Trevino holed an outrageous putt for a birdie. That was cause for generous congratulation, for golfers in the main are sincere in their compliments for other players' good fortune. The same thing happened on the 15th green and that was not quite so amusing. Jacklin had the first inkling that he was playing not only a flesh-and-blood opponent but a capricious supernatural spirit as well.

That feeling was reinforced with the power of a kick in the stomach at the next hole when Trevino had a difficult lie on a downslope at the back of a greenside bunker. He caught the ball thin and it flew low and fast from the sand, heading for the bogey territory over the green. The ball hit the flagstick squarely about three feet above ground level with a sharp bang and dropped into the hole. Birdie. Trevino roared with laughter at this extraordinary fluke but for Jacklin it was far from funny. It may have been funny in the sense of peculiar, to the point of incredible, but it was definitely not ha ha funny.

On the 17th green Trevino landed another long putt. Birdie. By now Jacklin was becoming fatalistic. It was obviously Trevino's day and there was nothing he nor anybody else could do about it. This run of luck must end sometime. Luck evens itself out in golf. Perhaps it would go the other way at the 18th.

Such indeed seemed to be the case when Trevino overshot the green and faced a difficult recovery shot. His chip was much too strong and 999 times out of a thousand that shot would have

found the rough on the far side of the green, possibly a pot bunker. Once again the ball clattered against the flagstick and dived into the hole. Birdie. Trevino's 66 gave him the lead by one stroke, with Jacklin's solid 67 dropping him into second place.

Trevino cheerfully admitted that all his closing five birdies had been the product of sheer, unadulterated luck of such boundless generosity that it proved God must be a Mexican. Jacklin had good cause to reflect that he had done a thoroughly professional job in keeping his game and spirits intact in the face of Trevino's windfalls.

On the last day Nicklaus duly made his move, shrugging off the caution which had directed his play for the opening rounds. Jacklin and Trevino heard the ominous roars ahead of them but they were absorbed in their private conflict. At least Jacklin had to contend only with a mortal golfer on this occasion, with no outside interference from partisan deities, and they were level as they stood on the 17th tee. Trevino hit a poor drive and was duly punished when his ball found a pot bunker. Muirfield probably has the most penal fairway bunkers in the world and it was impossible for Trevino to advance the ball far from this cavernous hazard. Jacklin hit a perfect drive. Trevino chopped his ball out into the fairway and then hooked his third shot into the rough, still a long way short of the green. Jacklin's approach left him within chipping distance and sitting pretty for a birdie. Trevino, on the other hand, would have to work hard to save his par and that prospect vanished when his pitch from the rough went through the green and finished in a dreadful sandy lie.

Jacklin counselled himself not to try anything too fancy. Safety does it. As a result of this slightly defensive attitude he left his chip shot 15 feet short. He was still firmly in the driving seat, however, for Trevino's problem was acute. Trevino later admitted to me that at this point he mentally conceded the Open to Jacklin. He had enjoyed more than his ration of luck for one championship. However, he could not walk up and shake Jacklin's hand and call it a day. The shot had to be played, the formalities observed. He took his wedge and made what in his reconciled frame of mind was a perfunctory chop at the ball. Possibly it was precisely because he was not trying too hard on the shot and swinging with no trace of nervous tension that the contact was perfect. The ball skipped onto the green and rolled sweetly into the hole.

The blood drained from Jacklin's face. His heart sank into his boots. What other clichés are there to describe his feelings? Oh yes, his world collapsed. He swore inwardly and passionately. It had started again. Destiny was on Trevino's side. That is no kind of thought to entertain as you set yourself to the putt which can win you the Open. Jacklin missed, the ball sliding four feet past the hole. He felt physically sick and missed the return.

In the space of a few moments a hole which he had played in masterly fashion from tee to green had cost him a six while his rival had chopped about like a hacker and come up with a par five. It was too much for the human spirit to endure.

Now Trevino showed the stuff of a true professional. He knew that Jacklin was mentally shattered and must not be given time to regain his composure. He ran to the 18th tee and cracked his drive down the fairway. Jacklin played the hole like an automaton for a listless five to Trevino's safe par.

Tony Jacklin is an ebullient creature and naturally resilient. After this crushing experience it took some time before he was his old gregarious self and rationalizing Muirfield as one of those things which happen in golf. Time heals most wounds but I believe that some part of Jacklin's psyche died on the 17th green on 15 July 1972, and that he was never quite the same golfer again.

Seven up, and down the hatch

Tony Lema was killed in an air crash in 1966 and it saddens me to hear the reaction of young golfers when his name crops up in conversation. Wasn't he the guy who blew a big lead in the World Matchplay Championship against Gary Player? What a travesty that a man's whole life should be reduced to a vague memory of 18 holes of golf. That epitaph is a grotesque betrayal of one of the finest golfers I have ever seen and it does less than justice to one of Player's finest achievements.

Lema was a debonair character but a combination of circumstances gave him a totally unjustified reputation. It is a fact that he won the 1964 Open Championship at St Andrews without having played a full practice round and it is a fact that he was labelled with the nickname Champagne Tony. It was therefore assumed that he was less than a dedicated professional, a man of such exceptional natural talents that he could win without really trying. Anyway, win or lose, there was always the party in the evening.

In fact, as anyone who understands professional golf must realize, Lema's seemingly effortless skills and relaxed approach to golf were the supreme example of the art which conceals work. But he did lose a match which he should have won and the story deserves retelling. Years after that fateful semi-final at Wentworth, Lema's manager, the gregarious Fred Corcoran, told me that Lema was being treated for a circulatory problem at the time, and that at lunch, when he stood seven up against Player after the morning 18 holes, he realized that he had run out of the pills which his doctor had prescribed. He thought he had a fresh supply somewhere in his luggage but there was no time to go and search for them. Besides, at seven up, it hardly seemed to matter if he missed his midday dosage.

Whether Lema's strength was seriously impaired by this omission nobody can say. What can be said is that the indomitable spirit of Player, and the manner of his play, would probably have prevailed against anyone on that extraordinary afternoon.

Player felt crushed at the end of the morning round. He had watched the crowd evaporate as they had drifted away from this foregone conclusion in search of more potent drama from the other semi-final. He himself knew that he was beaten and he dreaded the public humiliation which he knew must await him when the match resumed. Then, as he sat in the dining room of the Wentworth clubhouse, Player found himself growing stronger. He could not explain what was happening to him, either then or now, but it was a mystical, even spiritual, experience. My reaction to this recital was a cynical and unspoken 'Hogwash!' There was no mystery about it. Player's entire life had been a battle against hopeless odds. The scrawny, undersized kid with a hopeless swing had become so conditioned to beating the odds that by this time he actually needed adversity to stimulate his Napoleon complex. If there was no impediment standing in his path then perforce he had to invent one. In 1978 he won two tournaments in a row, the US Masters and Tournament of Champions, after starting the last day seven strokes behind. The reason he won was because everyone else in the entire world knew that such an outcome was impossible. That's how the world viewed the prospect of a Player victory against Lema.

Player pulled back two holes on the outward nine holes and those gains did not appear remotely relevant. After all, Lema still had a credit balance of five holes for the remaining nine holes. Lema missed the green at the short tenth and lost the hole to a regulation par. Player, brisk and dapper, a bundle of nervous tension, hit a gigantic drive at the next and reaped his due reward of a winning birdie. For the first time in the match Lema experienced the sickening feeling of being on a slippery slope.

Arnold Palmer rates the 13th as the best hole at Wentworth because of the need for absolute precision in judgement and execution of the tee shot to the hog's back fairway. The margin for error is acutely limited. Towering trees block out a second shot to the green if the ball is left, more trees await a mistake to the right on the other side of the dog-legged fairway. Player's drive found the area the size of a tennis court which represents the optimum site for the approach: Lema hit an ugly, low hook into the woods. He could only hack it clear for an unpropitious shot towards the green. Player hit a beauty. Lema's shot came up well short but if he could only hole his gigantic putt it might unsettle Player sufficiently to earn a half. Down went Lema's monster. Player judged the swing of his ten-foot putt to perfection and holed it. Psychologically that was worth more than a birdie.

They halved the next two holes and then Player gambled with his driver on the tight 16th, a natural one-iron hole if ever there was one. Lema felt that he could not afford to give Player too much advantage of length, Player having only a short-iron second to the flag. He reached for his three-wood and Player's trap was sprung. He had tempted his opponent into selecting a wooden club, younger brother of the club which had just let him down badly three holes previously. Lema's shaken confidence produced another hook and another win for Player.

On the 17th green both faced difficult putts and each man knew that, come what may, somehow he had to get that putt into the hole. Lema putted first and in it went. Now, unless Player followed suit, it would be all over. Player was well aware of the fact. Unless he holed out his supreme effort of will all afternoon would go for nothing. His putt dropped.

Both drove well enough at the last to give them a sight of the distant green on this winding par five. Lema's second was a disappointment, the ball coming up short of the green. Player hurled himself into his shot and watched in dismay as the ball rose over the line of trees alongside the right-hand side of the fairway. He listened for the ominous knell of ball striking wood. Instead he heard a tumultuous roar from the grandstands behind the green. The ball had safely carried the danger and had drawn back to the green, close to the flag.

Lema forgot that this 18th green, sheltered by encircling trees, is notoriously softer than the other 17. His chip was woefully short and Player squared the match. By now Lema was broken. His long approach shot at the first extra hole hooked away into a bunker below the green and the most famous victory, and equally notorious defeat, in the history of the World Matchplay Championship was complete.

It was, however, by no means the record reverse in major matchplay championships. That distinction belongs, I believe, to Al Watrous, who was beaten by Bobby Cruickshank in the US PGA Championship (when it was decided by matchplay) after being 11 holes up with 12 to play. Watrous was an ill-starred golfer. He looked to have the British Open Championship in his pocket on the 71st hole at Royal Lytham in 1926 when Bobby Jones pulled off what is probably the most celebrated single stroke in the history of the game. Watrous was so shaken by this remarkable mashie shot from Jones, now commemorated by a bronze plaque, that he three-putted and had to settle for second place.

As easy as falling off a log

There are times when golf is easy. These are rare and magical experiences, even for the finest players. The club seems to swing itself and the player is free to concentrate on plotting the destination of the shot. He visualizes the ball in the air and the next thing he knows there is the ball following that precise path. Everything he attempts comes off.

The experienced player is highly suspicious of these transcendental episodes. He is prepared to ride the wave of fortune for as long as it lasts but he is braced for the inevitable moment when the breaker must explode beneath his feet and deposit him head first onto a rock in a cloud of spray. He reminds himself that the Lord giveth, the Lord taketh away.

Young Denis Watson was intoxicated with euphoria in the Swaziland Open when it all started to happen. One minute he was grinding along for a possible finish in the top 20 and a modest cheque and then the birdies started. He had six in a row to take the lead with one hole to play. He felt that destiny had taken him by the hand and was leading him to a preordained victory. He was bewitched. All he had to do was select the right club and the spell would go on working.

In other words he was beautifully set up for one of those vicious kicks in the groin which so delight the warped sense of humour of the golfing fates. Watson's approach shot to the home green started off dead on line but a cat's paw of wind patted it off course, just sufficiently to direct the ball against the limb of a tree.

Thanks to meticulous planning by the dark forces of evil the ball met the branch at the precise angle to cause it to rebound into a bunker, in a difficult lie. Maybe a battle-hardened cynic could have thwarted the malicious plot by exploding the ball up to the cup for a winning four. Watson, in his innocence, was by now so conditioned to the feeling that his body had become possessed by the spirit of golfing genius that he made no attempt to take control of the situation. He set himself to the ball and waited for yet another miracle shot to happen.

Once again the club seemed to swing itself. The ball flew like an arrow right over the green and out of bounds. No doubt squeals of demented laughter greeted this stroke in the clubhouse on Mount Olympus. Watson was on his own again. He played out the hole in a dream and retains only a hazy recollection of the details. He thinks he finished with a nine.

Hush, hush – here comes the bogey man

Let us concede right away that the 15th hole of the Atlanta Country Club is a pig. It measures 448 yards down a fairway which angles sharply around a rocky outcrop with a creek snaking its treacherous course alongside this mini-mountain. Then, to rub salt into the wounds, the creek winds across the fairway in front of the green. It is, therefore, a critical driving hole – but great players are supposed to be sure drivers.

During the 1982 Pacific-Atlanta Classic the spectators might have been excused for questioning whether they were watching great players in action. After a storm delay, five of the six players who returned to the 15th tee were in contention: Larry Nelson and Keith Fergus at 16 under par, Raymond Floyd and Wayne Levi at 15 under, Peter Jacobsen at 14 under.

They were thus able to observe each others' play of this crucial hole and fall victim to the kind of mass hysteria which afflicts the lemming. One by one they hurled themselves over the cliff in a rare example of a group disaster.

Floyd hit his second shot into the creek for a double-bogey six. Levi drove out of bounds, found the creek with his second ball and eventually holed a ten-footer for an eight.

Nelson drove onto the rocky hill, pitched into the creek and three-putted for a seven. Jacobsen took six. Fergus drove among the rocks, pitched back to the fairway, hit a four-wood shot to the fringe, chipped to 20 feet and, greatly to his relief, holed the putt for a bogey five.

That bogey proved to be as valuable as Gene Sarazen's double-eagle at Augusta in the Masters. Fergus won the tournament on the first extra hole of a play-off with Floyd.

2

The wrong side of the law

The first thing we do, let's kill all the lawyers.

William Shakespeare, *Henry VI Part II*

'What a stupid I am'

Kel Nagle is known throughout the world of golf for his modesty, his unfailing good humour, his sportsmanship, his kindness and his reliability. When he won the Centenary Open Championship at St Andrews his victory was widely regarded as triumphant rebuttal of the adage that nice guys don't win, in much the same way that Roberto de Vicenzo's Open Championship was greeted seven years later.

It is therefore ironic that both these admirable men should have been the victims of gruesome encounters with the rules of golf. There was a ludicrous quality about the Nagle incident which allows us to look back on it with a wry smile, but in the case of de Vicenzo the passing of time does little to calm the initial feelings of outrage. It is a measure of the man that he himself shrugged off within moments the most savage disappointment to be suffered by a golfer of the modern era.

In the 1969 Alcan Golfer of the Year tournament at Portland, Oregon, Nagle was well placed after the second-best opening score, a 70, and he prospered again in the second round. However, his marker inadvertently entered his first nine-hole total, 35, in the space for the ninth-hole score. According to the rules, a golfer is responsible for the accuracy of the scores for each individual hole and it is no part of his duties to add them up and enter the total. If a player signs for a score higher than he actually took then that score has to stand. Since Nagle had signed his card the officials had no option but to accept that he had expended 35 strokes at the ninth, giving him a total of 105. Instead of being in position to challenge for the $55,000 first prize, Nagle was inevitably consigned to last place.

For de Vicenzo that rule about a player being responsible for the accuracy of the scores of each hole was again the cause of the problem. The last day of the 1968 Masters began auspiciously for the happy-go-lucky Argentinian. The Augusta National course was a picture in the bright spring sunshine and Roberto, two strokes behind the leader, celebrated his 45th birthday by pitching his approach shot straight into the cup at the first hole. The spectators massed behind the green sang 'Happy Birthday' and Roberto quickly settled into the rhythm of a winning round by making birdies at the next two holes. Destiny certainly seemed to have marked out Roberto for something special this day.

He is unique among great players in that on every shot his head comes up before the clubface contacts the ball, which makes it all the more strange that the faces of his clubs are worn smooth in an area the size of a shirt button on the precise sweet spot, testimony to the uncanny precision of his striking. (Actually, Andy Bean also looks up before he makes contact with pitch shots although I do not think he is aware of this peculiarity.)

De Vicenzo went out in 31, closely challenged by Bob Goalby playing behind him. The dramas and heroics of the golf are not strictly pertinent to this story. Sufficient to relate that he thought he needed to par the last hole for a 64 to tie Goalby at least, possibly to win. He made five. As he came off the last green he was asked to come quickly for a television interview. He signed his card and obliged.

A moment later his playing companion and marker, Tommy Aaron, received a jolting shock. He realized that he had inadvertently marked de Vicenzo's card with a four instead of the three which he had actually scored for the 17th. Likewise, not that it mattered in law, he had marked the inward nine holes with a total of 35 instead of 34 and the overall total of 66 instead of 65.

It was estimated at the time that nearly ten million people had watched every stroke of de Vicenzo's birdie on the 17th hole on the television, not to mention the eye-witnesses in his gallery. None of that mattered. The rules clearly state that no alteration may be made to a card after the competitor has returned it to the committee.

There was consternation and confusion as the dire facts slowly came to light, with Goalby completing his round and apparently finishing in a tie with de Vicenzo. Behind the scenes Bobby Jones and the tournament chairman, Clifford Roberts, had been searching to discover if there was any way in which this appalling injustice could be rectified. Apparently not. Rules are rules.

The incident was a disaster for Goalby who was in a subdued mood when we dined together that evening. He felt himself cast in the role of a man who has taken advantage of another's misfortunes to win the Masters and was desperately disappointed that he could not play-off with de Vicenzo and win the tournament fairly and squarely. It was a disaster for Aaron whose clerical error had cast him in the role of villain. It was a disaster for the Masters organization which had not ensured time and privacy for player and marker to check the cards thoroughly before signing them. Most of all, of course, it was a disaster for de Vicenzo, who took it better than anyone.

In his speech at the prize-giving he said: 'What a stupid I am,' and received a tumultous ovation of sympathy. The remark was a cleaned-up version of the remark he had passed to me when he first heard of the mistake, but the good-natured tone of exasperation was the same in both cases.

Good intentions and the road to hell

Golf encourages the habit of honesty because the game is not worth playing if you set out to cheat. If you are so minded, it is ludicrously easy to cheat at golf, for even an impure thought is enough to warrant disqualification. Hence golfers develop a deep respect for the rules and a pride in observing them in every particular. That, you might think, is a highly satisfactory state of affairs, as indeed it is, but this commitment to legality can lead the golfer into trouble.

Take the case of Tony Jacklin in the 1974 Open Championship at Royal Lytham. It was an emotional occasion for he had won the championship at Lytham five years previously. He was bidding to repeat that triumph when his ball ran into a rabbit scrape. He duly followed the procedure for taking free relief from such conditions, dropping two club-lengths (as the rule then permitted) from the nearest point which afforded relief.

When the dropped ball hit the ground it rolled down a slope into a much more favourable lie, a good four yards from the rabbit scrape. Jacklin, conditioned not to seek undue advantage from the rules, thought that there must be something wrong. After all, the purpose of the rule was to give relief from a rabbit scrape, not to provide the player with a perfect fairway lie yards from the trouble.

In this sporting and fair-minded spirit he picked up his ball and dropped it again near the rabbit scrape. His actions were observed and trained eyes scanned the fine print of Rule 22-2c: 'If a dropped ball rolls into a hazard, onto a putting green, out of bounds or *more than two club-lengths from the point where it first struck the ground*, or comes to rest nearer the hole than its original position, it shall be re-dropped, without penalty.'

Jacklin's ball had not rolled more than two club-lengths after it struck the ground. It was undoubtedly in a much more favourable position but it was also within that two club-lengths limit, and not nearer the hole. Therefore it was in play and by picking it up Jacklin incurred two penalty strokes. Jacklin was dumbfounded by the decision. His good intentions had snared him and rendered him liable to punishment. From that moment he ceased to be a force in the championship.

The Canadian Bob Panasuik came to grief in the US Open of 1965 at Bellerive because of similarly honourable motives. Like every good professional he held it to be one of golf's leading articles of faith that you never dropped a ball nearer the hole. That injunction is repeated over and over again in the Rules of Golf.

So when Panasuik had the embarrassing misfortune to overhit his long, downhill putt from the back of the green at the short sixth so that it ran into the pond, he automatically dropped his ball on the tee side of the pond, keeping the point where it last crossed the margin of the hazard between him and the flag. All perfectly kosher. He then fluffed his chip back into the pond. He dropped again, perfectly lawfully, pitched on and two-putted for an eight, having expended seven strokes in negotiating 30 feet of green.

But for his innate honesty in automatically searching for the correct spot to drop not nearer the hole, Panasuik overlooked the stroke and distance option. After putting into the pond, he could have dropped on the green at the point from which he had putted, under the stroke and distance provisions, and he would certainly have saved himself several strokes. Because such a procedure would have involved dropping nearer the hole, Panasuik simply did not think of it.

The referee's decision is final for the time being

Rule 11-2 states baldly: 'If a referee has been appointed by the Committee, his decision shall be final.' All clear? Any ambiguities there? Let us not go into the question of whether, in the interests of social justice, the rule might have been more happily expressed by 'his *or her* decision shall be final'. Golfers have enough problems with the lawmakers without tangling with the shock troops of the women's rights movement. As rules go, this one appears to be a model of clarity. Every rule, the authorities remind us, says what it means and means what it says. With that injunction ringing in our ears we might as well read the rule again just to make sure. 'If a referee has been appointed by the Committee, his decision shall be final.' It doesn't seem to leave much scope for loopholes, agreed? Very well, class, if there are no misunderstandings about what the rule says and what it means, we can proceed to today's little test. Hands up everyone who interprets Rule 11-2 to mean that if a referee has been appointed by the Committee, his decision shall be final.

Oh dear. I am very disappointed with you all. You may put your hands down and the entire class will remain behind after school and write out a hundred times: The law is an ass, a creature which the Rules of Golf Committee is unable to distinguish from its elbow.

Surely you realize by now that when a rule of golf says something it oftens means the exact opposite. Take Definition 31. This refers to a 'forward movement of the club' to define a movement which is patently *backwards*. Again, in the Appendices giving specifications for clubs and balls there is a provision that grips shall be substantially straight. Yet since the body which framed that regulation happily approves grips shaped like Coca Cola bottles, we can see that the expression 'substantially straight' is intended to mean 'extravagantly curved'.

On those rare occasions when the austere members of the Rules of Golf Committee let their hair down and repair for the evening to the Folies Bergères they may be overheard greeting the chorus with cries of: 'Get a load of those substantially straight figures.' Doubtless on the occasion of their weddings they solemnly vow: 'I take thee to my wedded wife, to have and to hold from this day backward. . . .'

By the same token, the word 'final' in Rule 11-2 does not mean final. Dear me, no. It is intended to convey no more than an opening bid at bridge, a preliminary suggestion advanced for the sake of further consideration, a tentative offering, a mere conversational gambit to start the discussion.

John Schlee is a literal-minded man who laboured under the delusion that final meant final. Thousands of golfers have fallen into this semantic trap. In the first round of the US Open at Oak Hill in 1968 Schlee hit his ball into a lateral water hazard. What he wanted to do was go back behind the hazard, keeping the point where the ball last crossed the margin between himself and the flag, and drop a ball under penalty, under the provisions of Rule 33-2.

The referee demurred. Schlee must either invoke the stroke and distance option, going right back to the point where he had played the errant shot, or he must drop on either side of the hazard as decreed by Rule 33-3. Schlee, believing the referee's decision to be final, complied.

In this case, whether or not the referee's decision was final, it was patently wrong, as the Committee cheerfully confirmed. 'Oh, yes,' they said, 'the decision was a load of hogwash.' (The form of words I reproduce is substantially accurate, meaning that I have made it up, but their meaning is faithfully preserved.) 'Not to put too fine a point on it, the referee was talking through his ear. Of course, Schlee had every right to go behind the hazard and drop under the provisions of Rule 33-2.' But the referee ruled that he could not do that: surely his decision, once given, was final?

'Final? Heck, there's no finality about final. Schlee could have lodged an immediate appeal with the Committee against that bum decision. Or he could have played another ball under Rule 11-5 and the Committee could have ruled on the case at the end of the round. It's too late now. You see, once Schlee accepted the referee's decision and complied with it, then the decision became final.'

With the benefit of that clarification, we might offer a suggestion to redraft the rule along the following lines: 'If a gullible dupe of a player acts on the decision of a referee, even though that decision is patently a load of baloney, then the decision shall be irreversible.'

Before his premature retirement from tournament golf to the domestic tranquillity of a club job, the South African Dale Hayes was one of the most powerful players on the world scene. In the 1974 Open at Lytham his strength it was the strength of ten because his heart was pure. Hayes was a staunch adherent to the spirit of the rules and sportsmanship and so, when he launched a massive shot into a tangle of rough among the sand dunes, he was meticulous about following the correct procedure.

'Take a note of the time,' he commanded his caddie, 'and tell me when we have searched for four minutes looking for the ball.' Players, caddies and spectators combed the undergrowth until the caddie announced: 'Four minutes is up, guv'nor.'

'Right,' said Hayes. 'You continue searching for the allotted five minutes, but, to save time, I will now go back to the spot where I hit that shot. Shout if you find the ball within the stipulated five minutes.'

Hayes walked back, identified the divot he had dutifully replaced after playing the previous shot and dropped another ball over his shoulder. Before he could select a club there was a shout of triumph from up the fairway. Hayes looked up and saw his caddie waving his arms and signalling that the errant missile had been located. Hayes picked up the dropped ball and hurried forward, played a recovery shot and continued his round.

Meanwhile the television cameras had been following the incident and in the comfort of the clubhouse an official drained his gin and tonic and pursed his lips. When Hayes completed his round the Inquisition was waiting for him. 'Under the stroke and distance procedure, the moment you dropped a ball that ball became the ball in play and your original ball was deemed abandoned. Therefore, it is our duty to inform you that you played a wrong ball from a wrong place, and since you did not rectify this error before making a stroke on the next hole, you failed to complete the stipulated round and, furthermore, signed a wrong score. Ergo, we have no option but to impose the maximum punishment prescribed by law. You are disqualified.'

Every now and then one gets the impression that rules officials regret that they cannot order a miscreant golfer to be shot at dawn but, of course, they were quite right. If a rule exists then it must be applied impartially. That is only fair to the other competitors and everyone knows where he stands. Ignorance of the law is no defence and in this case Hayes had no excuse and, to his credit, accepted the judgement without demur.

However, the literal approach to the regulation of golf, with no regard to mitigating circumstances, does lead to travesties of natural justice, as in the case of the Schlee incident and the disqualification of Roberto de Vicenzo in the famous scorecard disqualification at the US Masters.

Britannia waives the rules

There is a precedent for rectifying glaring injustice. On the 72nd green of the 1957 Open Championship at St Andrews, Bobby Locke had a cushion of three strokes and his ball, close by the hole, awaited the formality of the tap-in to give him the fourth championship title of his illustrious career.

First, however, his playing companion had to complete the round and Locke's ball lay on the line of his putt. Accordingly, Locke measured off one clubhead length and marked to the side. When it came to Locke's turn to putt out, the atmosphere of excited euphoria was almost palpable. Ten thousand voices around the green were primed to fanfare his triumph with a mighty roar.

At his customary measured pace, and with his face set in its usual solemn mask, Locke set his ball in front of the marker, put the marker in his pocket, studied the line, followed his unvarying routine of two practice swings and rolled the ball smoothly into the hole. Only then did he permit himself a smile as the crowd erupted in a vocal avalanche of congratulation.

At this point I might declare my position in the continuing debate on the morality of the use of television and film evidence to bring golfers to judgement. Far from seeing the television camera as a one-eyed snooper, I believe that film and videotape is often the best witness as to fact and, where appropriate, should be used as such. In this instance television had a full record of the wrong procedure unwittingly committed by the champion.

The committee considered the facts and weighed the circumstances. In due course the chairman, Mr N. C. Selway, wrote to Locke as follows:

My dear Locke,

You will already have heard from the Secretary of the Royal and Ancient Golf Club that the championship committee intend to take no action with regard to the incident on the last green which appears in the television film of the Open. Your winning score remains at 279.

A penalty may, in exceptional cases, be waived if the committee considers such action warranted.

This committee considers that when a competitor has three for the Open championship from two feet, and then commits a technical error which brings him no possible advantage, exceptional circumstances then exist and the decision should be given accordingly in equity and the spirit of the game. Please feel free to show this letter to anyone.

With all best wishes.
Yours sincerely,
N. C. Selway.

That enlightened letter, incidentally, is the only example I have ever seen in which a ruling body of golf refers to the spirit of the game. What a refreshing change it makes from the usual blind adherence to the letter of the law. Locke was deeply moved by the committee's humane handling of the case and he felt that his private gratitude should find expression in some overt gesture, some mark of humility which would daily remind him of his debt to the committee's compassion. For all his golfing career he had worn plus-fours on the golf course, and this mode of dress had become his personal trademark and something of an affectation on his part. From the day he received that letter he never wore plus-fours again.

A delicate chip from the fine print

For over 20 years Jack Nicklaus has set an example to his profession and not least in his mastery of the rules. He studies the rules, keeps up to date with amendments and sees the rules for what they are: both as a series of commandments enjoining

the golfer against certain actions, for example, Thou Shalt Not Improve Thy Lie, and as the golfer's Bill of Rights, conferring a wide range of privileges. Nicklaus is equally zealous in his commitment to both aspects of the rules.

He does not try to browbeat referees into giving him favourable decisions and his concern is to follow the correct procedure. By adopting this neutral approach he does not think in terms of getting a good drop or a bad drop because there is only one right place to drop and he takes it, good or bad. By the same token, he claims the full rights which the rules afford.

His knowledge of the rules was shown to good advantage in the third round of the US Open at the Olympic Country Club in 1966. His approach to the tenth green was strong and the ball rolled through onto an embankment. As he walked to the ball he bent down and threw aside a twig.

He took his stance and was about to settle to the shot when he suddenly jerked his club back. He looked up, noticed a rules official standing nearby and announced: 'The ball moved.' During a brief consultation the player and the official agreed that Nicklaus had not grounded his club so he was not liable to a penalty under Rule 27-1f (ball moved after a player had addressed it) since grounding the club is an essential ingredient of the address under Definition 1.

But the previous clause of this rule (27-1e) says that if a ball moves after the removal of a loose impediment the player shall be deemed to have caused the ball to move. Penalty: one stroke. The question now arose as to the position of the twig before Nicklaus threw it away. Had it been within a club-length of the ball? A committeeman standing by the green had watched the incident closely and volunteered information. 'It was about two inches in front of where your left toe is now.'

At this point Nicklaus's knowledge of the rules paid off. What is a club-length? After all there is a difference of about eight inches between the length of a driver and a putter. Since golfers normally seek maximum distance in measuring club-lengths, as in taking relief from ground under repair, they automatically reach for the driver.

Nicklaus pulled out his putter. The official nodded in agreement. The putter is a club and the length of a putter is therefore a club-length. Nicklaus measured from the ball and the putter was two inches short of where the twig had been removed. There was therefore no penalty.

It may be that someone will get an idea from this incident and wonder whether it might not be an advantage to carry one of those one-handed putters about the size and shape of a hammer. Would the referee accept a club with a ten-inch shaft to measure a club-length? As to that, the inquirer would have to obtain an official ruling from the appellate division of the Rules of Golf Committee. For myself, in the unlikely event that I were asked to officiate as a referee, I would not hesitate to disqualify a golfer the instant he produced such a putter, on the grounds that clubs 'shall not be substantially different from the traditional and customary form and make'.

Don't bother getting out your driver

Rule 37-5 states: 'The player shall start at the time and in the order arranged by the Committee. Penalty: disqualification.' What heartache those words have caused in their time. Down the years golfers have gone to extraordinary lengths to get to the tee in time but they have got no change out of the hard-hearted starter. One man yelled from a train which inconsiderately failed to stop at a station, that he would 'be there in a few minutes'. And he was, but he was still a few minutes late and that was that. Another tried to make up time after a storm-delayed transatlantic journey by chartering a light plane and buzzing the course, to indicate that he was on his way. Nice try, but sorry. Another tardy competitor poured out a catalogue of disasters which had interrupted his travels from New Zealand to St Andrews. 'What frightfully bad luck, my dear chap,' said the starter. 'I do hope that all goes smoothly on your return journey, which you are free to start at any time.'

Disqualification for late arrival is so common that I will limit myself to one incident, on the grounds that it created a much bigger furore than usual because of the victim, Severiano Ballesteros.

When Ballesteros arrived at Baltusrol, New Jersey, for the 1980 US Open Championship, he was universally regarded as one of the leading favourites. At the age of 23 he was the reigning British Open and US Masters Champion and in his brief career he had captured the national championships of Holland, France, Switzerland, Japan, Kenya, Scandinavia and Germany, several of them twice. He was, in short, the brightest shooting star in the golfing firmament.

Just exactly how he, and his manager, and his caddie (brother Baldomero) and the Spanish supporters staying at his hotel all failed to anticipate the danger of a late arrival remains a mystery. The starting time had been public knowledge for two days previously. Even Ballesteros's assiduous biographer could cast no light on this curious incident beyond the discovery that the manager, Joe Collett, had not followed his usual practice of giving Ballesteros a reminder of his starting time.

The traffic was heavy on the morning of that second day, as it always is during major championships but, although Ballesteros made much play of that fact at the time, it was clear enough on his arrival at the club that the young Spaniard was unaware of his starting time. Normal behaviour in such emergencies is for the player to dash from the car to the tee in his street shoes and drive off, often enough with a borrowed club and ball, while the caddie collects the equipment. Ballesteros went to the locker room and changed into his golf shoes in a leisurely manner and it was only when a British golf writer told him that he was overdue on the tee that he made a frantic sprint. He was seven minutes late and was disqualified.

Looking back on that ridiculous episode, Ballesteros is unable to offer any rational explanation of how it happened but he is graphic in recalling his reactions. 'People respected me as a champion and I knew I was a champion. Now I felt such a fool. It did not matter so much what other people thought about me but it hurt very much that I had to accept my own foolishness. I had behaved like a silly boy and I did not think I was a boy. It was a very bad feeling. I had to get away from there as fast as I could.'

Ballesteros is in good company among the legions who have been disqualified for being late but there is a select company of six golfers with the unique distinction of being disqualified for starting *early* in a major championship.

It happened in the US Open at Canterbury in 1940, during the era when the last two rounds were played on one day. Thunderclouds were building up as the six players had lunch and they decided it would be a good idea to get out again before the storm broke. Accordingly the threesome of Johnny Bulla, Porky Oliver and Dutch Harrison followed by Ky Laffoon, Duke Gibson and Claud Harmon ignored all warnings and teed off 28 minutes before their official starting times. Oliver had a 71 for a total of 287 and his disqualification at the end of the round was particularly shattering because he would have been in a play-off with Lawson Little for the championship.

Just a regulation par four

There comes a watershed period in the life of the golfer when the confidence and optimism of youth are replaced by a kind of death-wish. An accumulation of years of bad bounces, rubs of the green and untimely coughs at the top of the backswing produces a deep cynicism and we take a perverted satisfaction at being singled out by the fates for special treatment. If by any chance a shot across a lake pitches on the far bank we shout at the ball: 'Go on, roll into that bunker. No, you've got a better idea. Quite right, how silly of me not to suggest it. Roll back down the bank into the water.' With an expression of martyrdom we shrug our shoulders and press the flesh against our hair shirts. The unspoken message to our opponents is clear: 'You may win but it will be a hollow victory because Jack Nicklaus himself could not prevail against the hideous curse which afflicts me.' Malign fate provides a soothing balm for our self-esteem and thus we secretly rush to embrace our disasters. I have not been beaten by a flesh-and-blood opponent for nearly 20 years.

I was just getting into this syndrome when I came across an example of a golfer who could not recognize a disaster when his very life was imperilled by it. It made a deep impression on me and, in the hope that it might do likewise for you, I shall relate the story of this non-disaster.

This was back in the days when professional golfers knew their place. True, Walter Hagen and Henry Cotton had pioneered the emancipation of professionals by this time but, of course, not every pro could arrive in a chauffeur-driven Rolls-Royce and hob-nob with the Prince of Wales. The conditioning of centuries is not cast off overnight.

The one concession which the majority of professionals made

to the advance of social progress was to change their shoes in the locker room rather than the car park. For the rest they spoke only when they were spoken to, were respectful to the members and barely controlled the instinct to tug their forelocks at the approach of the captain. Five centuries of the doctrine that professional golfers should be seen and not heard was still observed by the pros of the old school to the extent that they rather overdid it. They wore clothing of muted autumn tints which, on the golf course, effectively camouflaged them and rendered them pretty well invisible. You had to follow their progress by listening for the oaths of the caddies. These days we would call it keeping a low profile; to them it was nothing more nor less than professionalism.

It so happened that two of the invisible and inaudible men of British golf were also the best players of the day, Neil Coles and Bernard Hunt. Naturally, they were frequently paired together. Christian names were never used in professional sport in those days and these two kept the late Henry Longhurst in a constant state of palpitation in his television commentary box.

On the occasion under discussion a tournament was being played in Yorkshire and Coles was playing with Hunt on a sultry, thundery day. Rule 37 permits a golfer to leave the course if he considers there may be danger from storms and that, I may say, goes double for golf writers. The press corps to a man assembled in its tent and waited for the heroes of the day to be paraded before them for interview. The fashion in sports journalism had just changed at this period from eye-witness description of what the writer saw on the course to what the players *said* happened.

The craze for quotes was pretty hard work, I can tell you. Writers and PGA officials went crazy trying to teach the golfers to speak. When you consider that James Braid uttered about ten words in public during a career which embraced the winning of five Open Championships you can see what we were up against. Coles and Hunt were duly shepherded into the tent after two excellent rounds. The press officer started with Coles.

'Par at the first?'

'Ugh.'

'Birdie at two?'

'Mm.'

'How long was the putt?'

'Grrr.'

'Longer than ten feet?'

'Mm yeah.'

'Shorter than 20 feet?'

'Ah.'

It was like opening oysters with a toothpick but it was raw material enough for the skilled reporters to fashion their first-person accounts. 'Balding Ryder Cup veteran Neil Coles fired a sizzling third-round 66 and quipped: "My putter was red hot and I'm going to lean it against a radiator overnight to keep it that way." '

Hunt was more articulate but equally uncommunicative. He studied his card and recited:

'Par, par, birdie, par. . . .'

Coles, who was still seated at the interview table recovering from his grilling, raised an eyebrow. He gave a discreet cough. Hunt paused and looked at him. Coles, who was beginning to get the hang of this new journalism, whispered: 'Aren't you going to tell them what happened at the fourth?' Hunt checked his card. 'Regular par – drive, four-iron, two putts.'

Say what you like about the British journalist but he can recognize a dog when it bites him in the leg. We pounced. 'What happened on the fourth hole?' We probed. We prodded. We coaxed. We cajoled. Bit by bit it came out. As Hunt was addressing his ball for the approach shot his club was struck from his hands by lightning.

'What did you do then?'

'I picked it up again.'

'But what did you *do*?'

'I hit the ball front left, about 25 feet.'

It was not the most electrifying quote you ever heard but it was a start.

International incident over a five-iron

It is not too difficult to find people who are so thoroughly conversant with the basic rules of golf that they can adjudicate on a point of law without referring to the book. There are two in New Jersey, at least two in transit with the American and

European professional tours, one in South Africa, several in St Andrews and, I daresay, one or two east of Suez.

But when it comes to the esoteric areas of three-ball, best-ball and four-ball matchplay then even these experts do not trust themselves to give judgement without looking it up first. There was a classic example of legal complexities at the 1971 Ryder Cup match at St Louis, Missouri, when Gardner Dickinson and Arnold Palmer were playing Peter Oosterhuis and Bernard Gallacher in the four-balls.

The actual incident was simple and there was no doubt or ambiguity about what happened. University students were engaged to caddie for the two teams that year and, naturally enough, they were delighted to be so honoured and very enthusiastic. The Americans had the honour on the seventh tee and after they had hit off Gallacher's caddie said: 'Gee, Mr Palmer, that was a terrific shot. What club did you hit?'

'Fav arn,' drawled Palmer courteously, for he appreciated the interest of the golf fanatic student and sought only to be helpful and friendly. The referee, an experienced PGA professional named John Conley, overheard this exchange and recognized that the conversation constituted a breach of Rule 9: 'A player may give advice to, or ask for advice from, only his partner or either of their caddies.'

It is well established that the seeking and giving of *information* is perfectly proper. If the caddie had asked, for instance, 'How long is this hole?' and Palmer had replied '208 yards' then no exception could have been taken to the exchange. But by asking which club had been used the caddie had, in effect, been picking Palmer's brain with all its accumulated wisdom and experience.

The issue is not affected by the fact that any professional golfer can see at a glance what club his opponent is using and can confirm that knowledge by observing the trajectory of the shot. Nor is it affected by the fact that Palmer answered the question and so, as you might think, committed an equal breach of the rule by *giving* advice: by the time the question had been asked an offence had been committed and the penalty was due at that moment. In law the hole was forfeit by the time Palmer made his reply. Nor is the issue affected by the fact that the caddie did not communicate this unlawful advice to Gallacher, nor that Gallacher was blissfully unaware of the entire conversation, nor that, far from selecting his five-iron, he was already addressing his ball with the four-iron and stepped away to change the club for a three-iron.

None of these points concerned the referee for the moment. All he knew was that a breach of rules had occurred and that he was duty bound to do something about it. He did what any sensible referee does in such circumstances: he took the problem to Joe Dey who was then Commissioner of the American PGA Tour and one of the greatest living authorities on the rules. The two of them roped in Joe Black, President of the American PGA, to add further authority and experience to the discussion.

Meanwhile the players, oblivious to this intense legal activity, had played out the hole in what they and everybody else believed to be a half in three. When it was ruled that the hole must be forfeited to the United States, Palmer indignantly protested that he did not want any part of being given a hole because of legal nit-picking. 'Why don't we just forget it?'

Incidentally, the Americans won that match by one hole and it was widely believed in some quarters that the incident had a knock-on effect throughout the British team and cost the visitors a famous victory in the entire match. Certainly the British captain, Eric Brown, a man given to speaking his mind without the prior benefit of having made it up, delivered himself of some undiplomatic sentiments.

Giving the decision to award the hole to the United States was one thing; documenting the tortuous process by which that decision was arrived at was something different. It took several hours to sort out a communiqué for public consumption. There have been slight changes in numbering of the pertinent rules since those days so I will refer to the current rules to trace the due processes of law which resulted in that fateful decision.

The questions which the committee had to determine were whether an offence had been committed: if so, whether the player was liable for the infringements of his caddie; if so, whether the player or the *side* was to be penalized: and what the penalty should be.

They started with Definition 2: ' "Advice" is any counsel or suggestion which could influence a player in determining his play, the choice of club, or the method of making a stroke.' That was clear enough. The fact that Gallacher was not influenced was immaterial; he could have been.

Now they moved on to Definition 26: 'A "referee" is a person who has been appointed by the committee to accompany players to decide questions of fact and of golf law. He shall act on any breach of Rule or Local Rule which he may observe. . . .' So the referee had no discretion to develop a convenient case of diplomatic deafness. He had been obliged to take action. But what action?

They cited Rule 37-2: 'For any breach of Rule or Local Rule by his caddie, the player incurs the relative penalty.' No ambiguity there, so they moved on to Rule 40-3h: 'A side shall be disqualified for a breach of . . . Rule 37-2.' Ergo, said the committee, the hole must be awarded to the United States.

I thought then, and still believe, that the committee got it wrong. All the other clauses in Rule 40 spell out in full when the player or the side shall be disqualified *from the hole* or *from the match*. This particular clause 3h is concerned with disqualification penalties and the first part of it specifies a *player* shall be disqualified from the match. . . . The second part of the clause lists the infringements for which the *side* shall be disqualified. The inference is inescapably that the two parts of the clause are simply distinguishing when a player must be disqualified from a match and when a side must be disqualified from a match. If it was the intention of the rule to restrict the disqualification of the side *to that hole* then the rule would have said so, like all the other clauses.

Mind you, the committee probably did everyone a favour by getting it wrong: they surely prevented a riot. If Eric Brown was in a truculent mood it was matched by that of Gardner Dickinson who was the victim of a ruling in his single with Harry Bannerman. Dickinson's caddie picked up his ball from beside the hole, in an obviously gimme position, when Bannerman wanted it left in position to assist the aiming of his own putt. The referee awarded the hole to Bannerman, who went on to win by 4 and 3.

Dis-order of play

In four-ball golf the rules about the order of play are varied in one important aspect. The ball furthest from the hole still determines which side is to play the next shot but the partners can choose which of their balls to play first. Tactical considerations thus arise, especially on the greens. It may well be that the player whose ball lies furthest from the hole will ask his partner to play first, to secure a par so that he can have a go at the birdie, or to give him an indication of how his putt may swing.

This rule produced an explosive incident during the 1969 Ryder Cup match at Royal Birkdale between Brian Huggett and Bernard Gallacher and the Americans Ken Still and Dave Hill. There was already considerable needle in this match, arising from earlier episodes of gamesmanship and rulesmanship, and on the seventh green Huggett commented to the referee that the Americans were putting out of turn. The referee had no choice but to draw this fact to the attention of the opponents, who chose to interpret this intervention as a deliberate attempt to make them replay a successful putt. A discussion of marked acrimony was cut short when Ken Still snatched his ball from the green, thereby conceding the hole.

If that incident does not appear to qualify for an anthology of disasters, then the sequel certainly does. The outspoken and intemperate remarks of the two Americans thoroughly alienated the crowd and the rest of the match was played out against a background of booing and shouted insults from behind the gallery ropes. If boorish behaviour at an international match does not qualify as a disaster then I do not know what does.

Water, golf's great intoxicant

It is widely known that water is wet, and fluid, and runs downhill, and that the physical properties of the water in one puddle are pretty much the same as the water in the next puddle. Nevertheless, the Rules of Golf include water in the general prohibition against testing the surface of a hazard just as if water came in as many varieties as sand.

Pray do not ask me what possible advantage a player might

gain by ascertaining the texture of the water in which his ball sits, or how he could possibly improve his lie by touching the surface with his club or hand before making his stroke, but there it is. Rule 33-1 is uncompromising on the subject and for explanation you must apply to the Rules of Golf Committee.

Playing the ninth hole of the 1967 Doral Open, Tommy Aaron led the field by one stroke and his tee shot at this par three finished in the shallows at the edge of a pond. Aaron managed to extract the ball from its watery resting place, chipped to the green and then two-putted for a double-bogey five.

Or so he thought. However, an eagle-eyed custodian of the law observed these proceedings and informed Aaron that he must add two penalty strokes to his score for the hole because his clubhead had touched the surface of the water on his backswing. Aaron denied any such thing but since a referee is an arbiter of fact as well as of law, there was nothing the player could do about it. Instead of winning the first tournament of his career, Aaron finished fifth.

Repair to meet thy doom

Denis Watson took a six-stroke lead into the final round of South Africa's Tournament Players' Championship and, although the pack closed up on his heels, he had enough in hand as he came to the last hole to start thinking in terms of his victory speech and to resolve that his deportment in front of the cheering crowds should reflect nothing but credit on himself and his profession.

His towering approach shot was right on the flag and that seemed to be that. He could afford the luxury of three putts if necessary. Life was indeed sweet. When he reached the green he saw that his ball had pitched short of the flag and the backspin had caused it to screw back and run just onto the fringe. No sweat. The shot was a cinch.

Watson walked up to the hole and as he retraced his steps he automatically repaired the ugly pitch mark made by the impact of his ball. The PGA laid a heavy stress on the responsibilities of professionals to set an example in observing the conventions and courtesies of the game. If only amateurs were equally meticulous in repairing pitch marks and smoothing bunker sand then golf courses would not resemble minefields.

The referee walked across to Watson. That was a nice gesture, to be first on the scene to congratulate him. 'You must add two penalty strokes to your score for this hole,' said the referee quietly. Watson's jaw dropped. He blinked, frantically trying to make sense of the jumbled emotions and thoughts which assailed him. The dominant feeling was fear and it was the worst kind of fear, the nightmarish fear of the unknown. What on earth had he done? 'Rule 17-1, improving the line of your shot,' said the referee.

Now Watson had to hole out with his chip shot to win. He did not even put the ball close.

Make a test of survival

The Rules of Golf have been formulated under the assumption that the game is to be played by rational people in conditions which, broadly speaking, are capable of sustaining human life. The regulations are, therefore, inappropriate to the President's Putter on two counts.

This venerable competition is a matchplay tournament for members of the Oxford and Cambridge Golfing Society which is limited to old Blues, or men who played in the annual University golf match during their undergraduate days. Since an Oxbridge education gives the alumni a flying start in life, they tend to become mandarins of commerce, government and the learned professions and, accordingly, do not find it easy to assemble en masse for a week of golf.

They decided early on that since they comprised the key elements of the nation's social, economic, administrative, legislative and spiritual life, it would be considerate, if the country had to come to a halt while they played golf, to choose a time when the country was paralysed anyway, by the weather and the traditional strikes in such key areas as road and rail transport, electricity and the distribution of petroleum spirit.

The Society thus decided to play for the President's Putter during the first week of January. To be sure, the members selected the links of Rye on the Sussex coast, which is as far south as it is possible to get without leaving Britain, but January is January. Down the years the Putter has been played in every extreme of winter weather. Thanks to Rye's proximity to the

English Channel the blizzards, hailstorms and hurricanes are often laced with brine and the saline atmosphere discourages snow from settling for long. Only twice, I believe, has it proved impossible to complete the proceedings at Rye, although frequently this consummation has been achieved at a fearsome cost in human suffering, not to mention scoring standards.

The competitors often appear muffled up in layers of wool, dressed more appropriately for an Arctic expedition than golf. The Society's motto '*Primus inter pares*' has been loosely translated as 'one portable heating stove between the pair of you'.

For the 1983 Putter the weather produced an extravaganza of a gale to add spice to the first round. The wind raged with such fury that the players had to fight with straining calf muscles to walk against it, and they were so buffeted at the address that the backswing had to be curtailed to a convulsive lurch and timed for a temporary lull in the fury of the storm. The half-topped shot came into its own, sending the ball skimming just above the surface of the fairways and pinging off the more obtrusive mounds.

These, then, were the circumstances which led to a dilemma quite beyond the normal scope of the Rules of Golf. Michael Reece was playing Greg Collingham and when they reached the fourth green they naturally removed the flagstick and laid it alongside the putting surface. As Reece was about to putt a sudden squall of extra ferocity lifted the flagstick as if it was a piece of straw and blew it across the green against Reece's ball.

Rule 34-3 imposes a penalty for a ball striking a flagstick, but makes no provision for the converse. The bizarre incident raised a nice point of sporting law, akin to whether a boxer should be scored a point for battering an opponent's fist with his jaw.

The players mutually agreed that the ball should be replaced without penalty and that for the rest of the round the flagstick should be lain on the downwind side of the green. This procedure was ratified in due course by the highest authority in the land and so, strictly speaking, the episode does not qualify as a disaster. However, at the Putter it is generally considered to be a disaster to win your match and have to endure another foray into the sub-zero maelstrom.

3

Bundles and bunches

I am disappointed by that stroke of death,
which has eclipsed the gaiety of nations
and impoverished the public stock of harm-
less pleasure.

Dr Samuel Johnson

The case for the abacus in golf

What it is to be young and strong and talented and ambitious. Philippe Porquier was a trainee professional, or assistant pro as he would be designated in America or Britain, and he was impatient to win his spurs on the battlefield of tournament golf. Finally his boss said to Philippe: 'You are still very young and inexperienced but these are conditions which can be cured quickly. I think you are ready to start the treatment. You may send in your entry to play in the national championship.'

'*Merci, monsieur le prof,*' replied Philippe gravely, his polite demeanour concealing a surge of inner excitement. He practised with renewed diligence and in due course set off for La Baule and the Ouvert de France. He acquitted himself with credit in the preliminary skirmishing and in the first round his scoring was neat if not gaudy.

At a long par five, dog-legging to the right up a stiff incline, Philippe impressed his veteran playing companions with a mighty drive and a cunningly shaped three-wood which left him a mere 40 yards short of the green, nicely set up for a birdie. His pitch shot made contact with the ball close to the heel of the club, catching it a glancing blow with the hosel. The ball flew diagonally right and out of bounds.

This shot is to golfers what Macbeth is to actors, proscribed by convention from polite conversation. A superstitious fear of contamination requires golfers to refer to this shot in oblique terms, such as a lateral, or squirter or merchant bank. Fie to such squeamishness, the shot Porquier hit was a SHANK.

He dropped another ball and took extra care over the stroke. This time the ball flew off at another sickening tangent into the rough by the boundary fence. His marker recapitulated this sudden turn of events in order to be sure of keeping track of the score.

Let's see – drive, fairway wood, O.B., penalty, another unmentionable – he is now playing six. Before the drama was to run its course he would wish that he had armed himself with an abacus. Porquier's next attempt disappeared through the fence and was never seen again. That made two more. By now Philippe was gripped by a rigor of fear and his eighth shot moved the ball only a yard or so further along the rough. Number nine went over the fence and his 11th attempt put him pin high but still 40 yards from the flag. Number 13 just had to be unlucky and his caddie disloyally remained out of bounds so that he would be handily placed to retrieve the next one.

The caddie guessed wrong. Philippe made further progress on his wide circuit of the green and now the out of bounds became less of a danger, unless he contrived to propel the ball between his legs. He did not do that but the ball continued to depart at right angles to his point of aim.

Philippe went through the pain barrier and out the other side. The fireball in his stomach had subsided to a dull ache. He apologized for unduly detaining his companions and resumed his convulsive hacks at the ball. I use the term 'the ball' loosely, you understand. Perhaps it would be more appropriate to refer to 'the latest ball'.

The first rough outlines of a plan began to form in Philippe's demented mind. A murmur of approval endorsed the wisdom of his tactics as he set himself to pitch his 19th shot in the direction of the next tee. The second part of the plan involved 100 per cent concentration on not shanking. Philippe did his damnedest not to shank and, sure enough, the plan worked. The ball shanked, darting sideways onto the green.

He smiled shyly in response to the applause which greeted this cunning stratagem. Two putts later and his name was enshrined in the record books as the perpetrator of the highest score for one hole in the history of the European Tour – 21.

The only way to play the hole

Every virtue has an obverse side to the coin and the dogged determination which we so admire in the best professional golfers can at times turn into the vice of sheer pig-headedness. It did so during the 1927 Shawnee Open when Tommy Armour decided that the correct tactic on a certain hole was to aim the drive tight down the right-hand side of the fairway and draw the ball back to the fairway. Armour put ten drives out of bounds before he proved his point and made a 'birdie' with the 11th ball. He was credited with a 22, if credit is the word, but later insisted his score should have been 23.

A plaque at Rancho Park celebrates the time when Arnold Palmer was moved to roll up his sleeves and slug it out with the ninth hole. That was his finishing hole in the second round of the 1961 Los Angeles Open and a par would have given him a handy 69.

The fairway of this notorious hole pinches in at driving range and the painfully accumulated local wisdom is not to mess with this baby. Lay up short with an iron and put your trust in the putter if you have ambitions for a birdie. Well, Palmer wanted a birdie and he was never much of a one for pussyfooting around with irons off the tee. No golfer in history ever broke out of jail more often with spectacular recovery shots and Palmer's only concession to the patent dangers ahead was to leave the driver in his bag and select his three-wood. The ball drifted out of bounds to the right.

Palmer snorted, pegged up another ball and let fly again with the three-wood. The ball drifted out of bounds to the left. Out of bounds is the Alcatraz of golf, the one jail nobody ever escaped from, but Palmer had now bracketed the target and felt he had the measure of the problem.

He stayed with the three-wood and whacked it out of bounds on the right. By now the ruddy hue around his gills was not entirely due to the Californian sunshine. He lashed another ball with the three-wood and hooked it out of bounds to the left.

His fifth tee shot stayed on the golf course, glory be, and he completed the hole in 12. At moments like this it is prudent to steer a wide berth around the victim. If perchance you happen to be in the locker room when he enters then it is recommended that you develop a fanatical interest in the notice board and peer unwaveringly at, say, the exhortation not take towels onto the golf course, making not the slightest sound or movement. Usually within about a quarter of an hour, when the maintenance men are discussing whether the door of the locker number 96 is beyond repair and you can hear the cold shower spitting and hissing as it meets superheated flesh, it is safe to tiptoe from the premises.

However, stern duty requires unfortunate evening paper correspondents to obtain instantaneous reactions for their dead-lines and Palmer was duly asked how he had managed to make 12. To his eternal credit he summoned up a massive effort of will and replied, not without an understandable abruptness: 'I missed my putt for an 11.'

The 13th hole at Estoril on Portugal's western seaboard also has an hourglass figure. It is an inviting hole, played steeply downhill and from the tee the golfer has a glimpse of the green. True the avenue between gnarled cork oak trees is treacherously narrow but the seductive message of the view from the tee is: 'Never mind the trees. If you get the ball up and flying, and if you catch it a real purler, then you can carry it over all the trouble right onto the putting surface for a certain birdie, maybe an eagle.'

Sebastian Miguel, one of the brilliant golfing brothers who pioneered the game in his native Spain, heard that siren voice during the Portuguese Open Championship and accepted the challenge. The rest is legend, and legends are notoriously un-trustworthy. It is sure that the wiry little Spaniard ran out of golf balls and had to beg fresh ammunition from his playing companions, including in desperation a yellow range ball. He also ran out of strength but not determination. Ball after ball was despatched out of bounds with a fine impartiality, distrib-uted equally to right and left. Everyone present was gripped by powerful emotions as the bombardment continued and this may account for a certain conflict among contemporary accounts of the incident. The circumstances were hardly propitious for ac-curate mathematics. Some survivors of the Estoril Massacre swear that Miguel hit 22 balls out of bounds before he found the green. Other eye witnesses stoutly aver that he hit 11 balls out of bounds and then holed a good putt for a score of 22.

By the time Miguel walked to the 14th tee he did not care and as far as the championship was concerned the actual tally was of no more than academic interest.

To inflame the spirit just dilute it with water

The 16th hole at Cypress Point is probably the most famous hole in the world, certainly the most photographed. In the realms of superlatives it may also be the most beautiful hole in the world, the most difficult par three in the world and the scene of the most rapidly rising blood pressure in the world, in terms of inches of mercury per minute per square yard.

Mind you, it is by no means the longest par three in the world for the linear measurement from tee to green is 233 yards. However, it provides an excellent example of the only known exception to Newton's law of motion. With all due modesty I must confess to the discovery of this important scientific deviation from the otherwise inexorable rule that $E = MV^2$.

The aberration occurs only in golf and so the revised version of Sir Isaac's law may be expressed as follows: The distance (E) a golf ball will travel is the product of the mass (M) of the clubhead multiplied by the square of the velocity (V) of the swing at impact, *except over water*. Porky Oliver was a noted victim of this vital qualification. He was a powerful man and a fine player, well capable of making the carry across the crashing Pacific breakers to the distant rocky promontory on which the green is sited.

He made all the right calculations of distance, judged the external effects of wind and weather to a nicety, selected the correct club and made solid contact with a smooth, unhurried swing. The ball fell short, smacked against the cliff and rebounded among the sealions.

Porky checked his programming data and, since the answers came out the same, he saw no reason for changing his routine. After all, he had confirmed that he had the right club. He made another good swing and the same thing happened. At that time, I should add, I was engaged on research into the magnetic attraction of trees and had not yet developed my suspicions

about water hazards into so much as a working hypothesis. Poor Porky could have no idea that he was bucking a law of nature. Two more perfectly judged shots found their watery destination before Porky took what was clearly, in his mind, too much club and landed his ball on terra firma. Forget anything you may have heard about fat people being of calm disposition; that does not hold in golf either, especially after four shots into the briny. He finished the hole in 16 irate strokes.

Dry but not necessarily home

Disaster likewise overtook Henry Ranson on the 16th at Cypress Point. In his case the tide was out and his ball finished on the beach at the foot of the precipitous cliff. He clambered down, inspected the lie and came to the conclusion that he could play a cut-up shot and make the green.

It took quite a long time and a vast expenditure of energy to shake Ranson's conviction that he could play a successful recovery shot from the beach. After 16 attempts the message got through and he picked up his ball.

With problems of this severity to be surmounted on the ocean voyage, it might seem reasonable to expect that once a golfer has successfully achieved the sanctuary of the narrow promontory his difficulties should be over. Perhaps the green will be receptively dished, to gather the ball into the flag. Surely there will not be any tiresome rough grass around the perimeter of the putting surface. Any golfer who entertains such thoughts of benevolence is in for a shock. Dr Alister Mackenzie was a leading exponent of the *Pilgrim's Progress* school of golf-course architecture and, in the interests of purifying the golfer's soul, he provided further challenges on the road to salvation.

It is called ice plant. It is very attractive to the eye, covering the ground in a dense mass of thick fronds much the shape and size of your little finger. On first acquaintance they look soft and succulent and you might wonder whether a handful popped into boiling water and then drenched in butter might not melt in the mouth like asparagus. The ice plant's air of sweet innocence is enhanced by attractive purple flowers. The first time I found my ball nestling in a clump of ice plant I was reluctant to sheer away a swathe of that luscious vegetation with my brutal wedge.

It would be committing an act of vandalism. Accordingly I essayed a delicate stroke, seeking to pick the ball cleanly without desecrating this wonder of nature. The leading edge of the club hit one of those fronds an inch from the ball and recoiled a foot. The ball did not even shudder. After four increasingly vicious swipes I retired with a sprained wrist.

You see, as I may have hinted, the appearance of the ice plant is deceptive. Those fronds are actually the consistency of chopped-up fan belt, tougher even than the calimares in bouillabaisse. A hand grenade would not shift them, as Hans Merrell eventually concluded during the 1959 Bing Crosby National Pro-am. Merrell flicked, hit, punched, hacked, slammed, whacked and lambasted with increasing expenditure of energy. It would not be fair to say that he got nowhere. He moved the ball about in the ice plant but it was half an hour before his ball was free of its clutches. He holed out in 19 strokes, a record in the catalogue of horrors at the 16th. Still, these examples of black comedy increase the lustre of Bing Crosby's hole-in-one, one of two aces ever recorded on this blessed corner of the Monterey Peninsula.

'Hang on a minute, guv'nor; you'll wear yourself out.'

Perhaps the most rewarding side of a life devoted to writing about golf is to watch the game mould the characters of the players. The great champions are regarded as models of deportment on the course, and rightly so, but when I see a Tom Weiskopf calmly hitting five balls into Rae's Creek in front of the 12th green at Augusta, his emotions held firmly in the vice of self-control, or Jack Nicklaus curtly acknowledging a doubtful ruling and getting on with his game, I cannot stem the flood of memories which spring from the past.

No British golfer of recent times has acquired such an aura of sober statesmanship as Neil Coles. As chairman of the tournament committee he set an impeccable example to his fellow players and presided over disciplinary hearings with the demeanour of a bishop wrestling with a knotty point of ecclesiastical dogma.

No golfer ever fought and won a more savage battle with his turbulent nature. I treasure many memories of Coles and his regular caddie, Arthur Maidment, who was known universally in British golf as 'Chingy'. At Sunningdale they had one of their regular disagreements over clubbing and this altercation resulted in the ludicrous spectacle of Coles tugging furiously at the head of his four-wood while Chingy tenaciously clung to the grip and tried to pull the offending club from his master. They looked for all the world like two starlings engaged in a tug o' war with a worm. Finally Coles gained possession of the club, brute strength prevailing over the ageing Chingy, and he hit a glorious shot from deep heather to four feet from the flag. He glared at Chingy with an expression compounded of triumph and contempt as he slammed the club back into the bag. Chingy, never lacking in spirit and determined to have the last word, replied fiercely: 'You would have been closer with the three-iron!'

However, that incident hardly qualifies as a disaster. For that we must return to the days when Coles was setting out on his illustrious tournament career and seeking, as a young assistant professional, to qualify for the old *News of the World* Matchplay Championship. The qualifying course was Dunstable Downs and Coles selected his nine-iron for a par-three hole of 126 yards. It turned out to be one of those shots for which the gulf between triumph and disaster can be measured in inches. In this case, six more inches of carry would have pitched the ball onto a downslope and sent it rolling close to the hole. As it happened, the ball plummeted under the overhanging lip of a cavernous bunker. With the benefit of more than a quarter of a century of experience, Coles now recognizes that it was physically impossible and sheerest folly to try to advance the ball directly towards the flag from this desperate lie. Youth sees such challenges differently, however, and Coles set himself for an almighty blast at the ball. Naturally, he succeeded only in driving the ball deeper under the lip. His second attempt made matters worse and by now all his capacity for rational thought had drowned in the rising tide of anger which engorged his features. He would get this ball out even if it meant demolishing half the golf course. He resumed his labours which resembled a frenzied experiment in open-cast mining. Sand flew by the bucketful. Turf bespattered the green. The ball remained in the bunker. After five or six thunderous blows his caddie shouted: 'Hang on a minute, guv'nor. You'll wear yourself out. Take a rest.'

Coles duly paused briefly before resuming his furious on-slaught. It took four or five more blows before his anger subsided through physical exhaustion.

Like Napoleon on the road to Moscow, he finally allowed the realities of the situation to penetrate his consciousness. He turned and pitched back towards the tee, then chipped to the green and holed out. He marked himself for a 16 although on later reflection he felt he might have over-estimated the extent of his trauma by a stroke, not that it mattered then or now.

With ammunition running low . . .

The year 1982 started badly for Ben Crenshaw. There was nothing in particular wrong with his game, just a general malaise of the kind for which a doctor would prescribe a tonic and advise a few days' rest if it occurred in a human patient. Being unable to put his finger on a specific weakness, the frustrated Crenshaw lost confidence and began mucking about with his clubs, having shafts changed and generally tinkering with them, in the hopes of finding the lost sparkle. His indifferent form started him worrying about making the qualifying cuts and that in turn put him into a defensive frame of mind. The experience brought home to Crenshaw just how fragile is that combination of con-fidence, outlook and skill which is expressed in the word 'form'.

He was therefore considerably encouraged when the dire downward spiral reversed itself in the first round of the Heritage Classic at Harbour Town, one of the most demanding courses of the US Tour and made even more difficult on this occasion by a frolicsome wind. A solid drive begat an iota of confidence and that assurance begat a good putt and, although not produc-ing spectacular figures, Crenshaw felt it all coming back, like a dry sponge absorbing nourishing moisture.

In the last round he was two over par for the tournament after 13 holes, good going in the rough conditions, and he stepped onto the 14th tee with the air of a man from whose shoulders a heavy burden has been lifted. He liked this 14th hole, a short par three to a small green, with a lake on the right. It is a hole to separate the sheep from the goats and Crenshaw was slipping confidently into his accustomed role as a goat. He had played the hole in all its moods and had never needed more than a punched five-iron into the type of headwind he now faced. On this occasion, however, he felt that the conditions called for what the pros call a knock-down shot, with a four-iron.

In plain language, that means playing the ball from further back at the address and keeping the hands slightly ahead of the clubhead at impact, with a short back-lift. So much for the theory. In the event the ball ballooned in the wind and tailed away into the lake. He tried again, same shot, same club. This was almost what he intended but just failed to make the distance. Splash. The third attempt was never in with a chance and joined its fellows in the lake. Number four reduced the shocked gallery to stunned silence. The spectators did not have the heart to raise even a sympathetic groan as the ball plopped into the water.

The caddie dug into the bag for a new sleeve of golf balls. Crenshaw put away the four-iron and took out the three. He hit a solid shot over the green, chipped from an unpromising lie to eight feet and holed the eight-foot putt for an 11.

Crenshaw then took eight at the next hole and, in his own words, finally settled down to finish the round with three bogeys for an 87 and a total of 306.

A watery grave

Many careers start inauspiciously and none more so than that of Scott Simpson. When he turned professional in 1977 he was confidently expected to breeze through the qualifying school tournament for his player's card. After all, he was the dominant amateur golfer of his day, NCAA Champion and one of the heroes of America's Walker Cup team with three victories in three matches.

Nothing he had encountered as an amateur or, indeed, that he was to meet in his brilliant professional career, compared with the tension of the qualifying school over the treacherous Pinehurst No. 4 course. The pressure came mainly from not knowing what standard of golf was needed and Simpson made the mistake of setting himself too high a standard, as he later realized. He felt that he had to make quite exceptional scores to qualify for the precious pasteboard which would give him the entry to the American professional Tour. This business of having to force a score, rather than just letting it happen, put him under a heavy emotional strain which was not helped by taking four putts on the sixth green in the first round. A birdie at the 11th got him back to level par but even at this stage he was feeling slightly shell-shocked.

The 12th hole is a par-five around a lake which cuts into the fairway, allowing the possibility of reaching the green with two really strong wood shots. Simpson went for a big drive and, as so often happens when straining for a few extra yards, pulled his drive. The fates were with him. His ball stopped on the bank of the lake about four feet from the water. Even so he had to stand with his feel well below the ball for his second shot.

He assessed his situation. He had two choices, either to pitch about 100 yards up the fairway, leaving him 220 yards over water to the green; or he could fly the ball 170 yards over the water and the play a short shot to the green.

For the birdie-hungry Simpson, the second option seemed the better bet. He took his three-iron to give him a good margin for error and caught the ball fractionally thin. It splashed into the lake. He had to drop a ball in the same spot and this time he selected his four-iron to get the ball flying higher. Again the contact was high on the ball and it buried in the oozing mud on the distant bank. He was shattered, unable to believe what was happening to him.

He stayed with the four-iron for his third attempt to get over the water and his heart sank as he watched yet another water spout as the ball fell short. He was numb and beginning to suffer from irrational fears that he might run out of golf balls. He was no longer disposed to dispute the advice of his wife, Cheryl, who was driving his golf cart. He dropped yet another ball, pitched out to the fairway, hit a good shot near the green, chipped on and two-putted for 12.

Simpson played out the round in level par but he was utterly depressed, embarrassed and shocked at his own stupidity. He felt that he had blown his career and that his life was a failure. He had failed both as a man and a golfer. That night he cried. It was some time before he could put the incident into true perspective and laugh at himself for what had been no more than a bad decision.

Donner und Blitzen – und Blitzen und Blitzen und Blitzen

The second highest score recorded in the 1950 Open Championship was compiled on the shortest hole in championship golf, the 126-yard eighth, or Postage Stamp, at Troon. For the young German amateur, Hermann Tissies, the black comedy started conventionally enough when his tee shot failed to find its tiny target and the ball pitched into one of the three bunkers which guard the green.

There is an endless and lively debate among the members of what is now Royal Troon as to which of these three bunkers carries the greatest potency for driving a golfer out of his wits. Technically they are all pot bunkers in the finest John Knox tradition of suffering being good for the soul. By the time he had completed the hole Tissies was something of an authority on the degree of difficulty of each bunker because he had been in all three of them. His vote goes to the bunker from which he needed five strokes to play into one of the others. In total he played nine bunker shots and, in the circumstances, he can be forgiven for taking three putts for his score of 15.

He went on to run up a score of 92 and it might be thought that oblivion awaited the recipient of such a comprehensive licking by the Postage Stamp. Far from it, the incident made Tissies famous and he went on to make a successful career in golf. As a businessman.

Come hell or high water – and plenty of both

Chivalry forbids identifying the lady in question but the prize for the biggest bundle in a serious competition probably goes to a competitor in the qualifying round of a women's tournament at the Shawnee club. As it happened the number of entrants was exactly the same as the number of qualifying places but it was decided to hold the qualifying round anyway since prizes had been put up for it. That decision was to provide a bleak footnote in the annals of golf.

Our anonymous heroine was probably not in line for one of the special prizes when she came to a short hole with a stream running in front of the green. And she was certainly out of the running for a silver spoon to commemorate finishing as top qualifier a few minutes later when she plopped her tee shot into the water.

Do not tell me that she could have dropped another ball short of the water and pitched into the hole to save her par. This was a player brought up in the stern tradition of playing the ball as it lies, no matter what. Come hell or high water she would get a club to the ball without recourse to effete legal concessions. She and her husband climbed into a boat and rowed out to the floating ball. She stood in the prow, her club raised like a harpoon, and called navigational instructions to her spouse. 'Port your helm,' 'Stop engines,' and 'Slow astern.' When the craft was manoeuvred into position she lashed at the ball, sending up a waterspout which drenched the two of them.

Sad to relate, her efforts were shabbily rewarded. As the frantic pursuit continued she gritted her teeth and became, if truth were known, slightly obsessive. She would get that ball out of the water if she died in the attempt. Most of us lesser mortals would surely have cut our losses after about 20 or 30 attempts but here was the true frontier spirit in action.

She had to complete the course in order to qualify – and she was going to complete the course her way, come what may. Pedants may argue that technically the ball was out of bounds after the first hundred strokes, because by now the boat had progressed a mile and a quarter downstream, and then, in triumphant vindication of the exhortation that if at first you don't succeed then you should try, try and try again, she cracked the problem of how to hit a golf ball from water. She cracked it all too well, for her mighty swipe sent the ball deep into a wood.

The mariners made landfall and continued the chase on foot. As pedestrians they got on much better and she eventually holed out on her 166th stroke. At something in excess of 3500 yards it had been quite a par three.

No ordinary water-hole

Water exerted its baleful influence in establishing the highest number of strokes, 19, ever taken for one hole in the US Open Championship. (In Britain the record was set in the very first Open, in 1860, and stands at 21 strokes. Rule Britannia.)

The par-four 16th at Cherry Hills was the scene of those 19 tragi-comic strokes during the 1938 championship, and the hero of the hour was one Ray Ainsley of Ojai, California. The front of this green is protected by a fast-running stream and this proved to be the resting place of Ainsley's ball, except that it did not rest. The strength of the current moved the ball along and Ainsley had to leap about in the water in spritely fashion, like a Samoan spear-fisherman attempting to transfix a restless carp, and make a swift slash at his quarry when it came momentarily to rest. Within moments, and the water dance seemed interminable, Ainsley was soaked and spattered with sand but you had to hand it to him: he was game.

Finally the ball settled against a propitious sand bar and Ainsley nailed it. He made sure of putting plenty of zip into the shot and the ball, as if frantic to escape further punishment from murderous assault, soared from the deep like a Polaris missile. It sought safety in the depths of a bush beyond the green.

Ainsley tracked it down to its lair and resumed his exertions, sparing neither himself nor the ball in belabouring it from its sanctuary. His perseverance was eventually rewarded, the ball popped onto the green, and was duly chased into the hole on the 19th stroke.

And some have disaster thrust upon them

At an early stage in the researching for this book I began to question the notion that some people are disaster-prone. That is to say, I rejected the idea that walking disaster areas are exceptional. Disasters of greater or lesser severity are the norm for golfers. The exceptions are those rare golfers who are immune to disaster. When I asked Peter Oosterhuis, for instance, to relate his worst golf-related experience he cudgelled his brains for 24 hours. He reviewed 15 years of almost daily competitive golf and could not recall one interruption to his serenity. All he could offer was an incident during the Juan Fangio period of his youth when he was driving at excessive speed to the Royal Lytham club for the 1974 Open Championship. The car skidded and Oosterhuis judged, wrongly, that there was an escape route between a tree and a telegraph pole. A jovial bobby, Police Constable No. 57 as Oosterhuis recalls, said: 'We can't have you late for your game, sir. You cut along and leave me to deal with the car.' Oosterhuis and his passenger, Bobby Cole, had bloody noses and made an incongruous pair as they covered the last hundred yards of their journey on foot, humping their golf bags, but the episode hardly causes a flicker of the needle on the disaster-meter.

Tsuneyuki Nakajima, on the other hand, has twice registered a maximum and almost broken the instrument. In the 1978 US Masters the brilliant Japanese professional drove into the creek which snakes along the side of the wood bordering the fairway. It is a common error on this hole because the player is obliged to flirt with danger if he is to put his ball into position to go for the green with his second shot at this par-five. He dropped out under penalty and played a good shot to within 100 yards of the green. Now he needed a delicate pitch because the flagstick was near the front of the green, just beyond that same creek which inconveniently crosses the fairway at this point. He pitched into the creek, in a position from which it was reasonable to try a recovery shot.

Unfortunately, he did not make it and the ball rebounded from the bank, hitting him on the foot for two penalty strokes. He handed the club to his caddie who dropped it into the water, occasioning a further two penalty strokes. Not surprisingly, his next pitch shot contained a slight element of vented frustration and the ball responded by flying over the green.

There is a distinct emotional pattern in these catalogues of disasters. For at least the first two damaging shots the player, if he is a good one, takes it in his stride and concentrates on containing the disaster. Then, as the horrors mount so does his gorge. Depending on the extent of the cataclysm there now comes a point where the emotion drains away and the player picks up the tattered shreds of his rational faculties and plays out the hole quietly with his spirit crushed. Nakajima chipped and two-putted for a 13 and no doubt, possibly the next day, he reflected that in golf luck is guaranteed to even itself out. That thought has sustained golfers ever since man first took a rudimentary club into his hands and saw his pebble take a bad bounce and miss the rabbit hole. Of course, as an experienced pro, Nakajima knew that this process of evening out the luck was not instantaneous. Those eight strokes of misfortune would not be restored by the fates in one week, or even a month, but over the course of the year he would be favoured by equivalent good fortune. Perhaps he would get his due recompense in another major championship. Nothing would suit him better than an eight-stroke bonus in the Open Championship in three months' time at St Andrews.

Well, he was still waiting as he approached the end of the third round. Luck or no luck, he had played well enough to establish himself right up among the contenders and when he hit the green with his approach to the treacherous 17th, the Road Hole, the last of the potential dangers was behind him. With a fairway 300 yards wide, the 18th hole offered a par at worst, with every possibility of a birdie. For this round at least he was virtually home and dry.

In golf there is no such condition as being home and dry. Nakajima rolled his putt up the green and watched in dismay as the slope directed his ball much further to the left than he had anticipated. It ran on and away and on and away and trickled into the Road Bunker. Now, even for a master sand-player, the Road Bunker presents an intimidating recovery shot. A fraction too strong and the ball is shrugged off the narrow, hump-backed green onto the road. Nakajima must avoid that fate at all costs and play an extremely delicate shot. It was too delicate. The ball stayed in the sand.

Exactly the same considerations obtained for the next shot. Exactly the same result.

At the fourth recovery attempt he made the green. Perhaps we should say that he regained the green he had been on four shots previously. Inevitably, he two-putted. That added up to 9 and for the second time in the space of three months he had been eliminated from a major championship by a bizarre disaster.

On the basis that the luck evens itself out, he must now be due to win a major championship with a final round containing 13 holes-in-one.

Watch the birdie, watch the fireworks

Photographers are people. They have to make a living. These are objective facts although there are times when they would be violently challenged in the locker rooms of golf tournaments. The problem arises because on occasion editors give golf assignments to photographers who do not know a brassie from a banjo and are equally unaware that tournament golfers are so highly strung that they make thoroughbreds appear like three-toed sloths.

Popular and famous golfers are the main victims of predatory photographers, obviously enough, which explains why Arnold Palmer was once dismayed when a cameraman walked into a bunker with him and settled happily in the sand alongside the ball, in position for a dramatic close-up. It also explains the hunted look in the eyes of Tony Jacklin as he scans the gallery before a shot.

During the 1982 Martini International at Lindrick Greg Norman was approached by a photographer with a request for an action shot. Sorry, said Norman, but he preferred no clicks until the ball had safely departed. In that case, said the photographers, perhaps Norman would hit a second drive off the 17th tee purely for photographic purposes. That, said Norman, would be illegal; please wait until after the round.

Norman had just made three birdies in a row and was intent on getting two more. He immersed himself in concentration to rip a big one down the fairway of the 397-yard hole, which would leave him a flick and another good birdie chance.

Dedication, application, and the nerve to seize opportunities when they present themselves are virtues of tournament golfers. These same qualities are also the hallmark of the photographer. At the top of his backswing Norman was transfixed by a click. In his state of heightened sensitivity the click was magnified to the volume of a pistol shot. Norman jumped and the ball hooked into trees, bushes, long grass, creepers and ferns, into a natural setting of such luxuriance as to move poets to rapture. It was what golfers call clag, or rubbish.

Norman found the ball and that in itself was something of a triumph. For most of us the obvious implement to extricate it

would have been a front-loader but the powerful Norman felt that forward progress lay within his powers if only he could negotiate the intervening branches. It was worth a chance. Moments later he reflected that perhaps it had not been worth the chance; the ball hit a branch and fell into what was beyond peradventure an unplayable lie, regardless of the golfer's bicep development. He dropped and moved the ball a few feet with his next shot, into another impossible position. This time his drop finished in his previous divot scrape, which resembled a deep trench. His next shot snagged in the undergrowth and tried to hide. There was nothing for it but to take another penalty drop. His next attempt made solid contact on the clubface – and also on a branch, the ball striking the bough at the precise angle to redirect it at about 100 miles an hour straight downwards into the thicket.

With an air of resignation Norman dropped the ball again and pitched it safely out sideways to the fairway. By this time he was hardly in the right frame of mind for precision golf and his approach missed the green. He chipped on and took two putts. Keen students of the rules of golf with a mathematical bent will be able without much difficulty to work out his score for the hole. It came to 14.

4

One of those days

I never had a piece of toast,
Particularly long and wide
But fell upon the sanded floor,
And always on the buttered side.

James Payn

When Gary had to take it on the chin

In 1955, on the strength of winning the Egyptian Matchplay Championship, Gary Player made his first trip to Britain. It was a hand-to-mouth tour for the teenaged South African, getting as much mileage as he could out of every penny by living in cheap digs, hitch-hiking where he could and subsisting on such fare as chip butties and the occasional veal pie in order to husband his dwindling resources.

It was therefore a matter of immense importance to him when he prospered during a minor tournament in Huddersfield and glimpsed a vision of first place. It was not much of a prize but to the impecunious Player it loomed as a fortune.

On the last hole he was told that he needed a four to win. Right, thought Player, desperate situations call for desperate measures, and he pulled out his driver and let fly. The tendency to hook with the driver, which was to plague him throughout his coming illustrious career, carried the ball right against a stone wall.

He reasoned that his only chance was to bounce the ball off the wall. Like a snooker-player calculating the angle of a cushion shot, Player determined the exact spot from which his ball would ricochet to the green, leaving him two putts for a square meal and an extension of his trip. He smashed as hard as he could into the ball, which struck a projection, rebounded and hit him on the chin, knocking him out cold.

When he recovered, he chipped on and holed the putt for what, in his understandably confused state, he believed to be a winning four. His playing companion had the unhappy task of reminding him that he had incurred a two-stroke penalty when his ball struck him. His scorecard for the hole was six. If that was rubbing salt into his wound, it was nothing to what was to come. He then learned that a five would have won the tournament for him. A five! Had he known that on the tee he would have played the hole quite differently – and to this day he insists that nothing would have been easier for him than to get down in five strokes on that closing hole.

Is there a frogman in the house?

A birdie would be nice but par was essential. Curtis Strange had calculated that he needed a four to qualify for the final two rounds of the 1980 Inverary Classic and as he walked off the eighth green (he had started at the tenth) he was calculating how best to tackle the narrow ribbon of 445-yard fairway, with water the entire length of the hole on the left, trees down the right and a bunker sited just at driving length. Three-wood off the tee and then, depending on how well he hit his tee shot, maybe a smooth seven-iron to the front of the green for an easy uphill putt. . . .

In order to reach the ninth tee the players had to cross a bridge with a low parapet, no more than a curb, really, over a wide canal. A press of spectators was crossing the bridge in both directions, and as Strange and his caddie were halfway across, the caddie was jostled. With the 50-lb weight of the golf bag on his shoulder, the top-heavy caddie keeled dangerously. Strange grabbed his arm and dug his spikes into the concrete. Splash! Splash! One by one the clubs slipped from the bag into 15 feet of water. All the woods went, followed by most of the irons. As the bag emptied, so the weight decreased and Strange was able to return the caddie to the vertical. They negotiated the bridge and took an inventory of the clubs remaining in the bag. Two-iron, three-iron, five-iron, putter.

The parlous position of being a borderline candidate for the cut had stretched Strange's nerves far enough, and the tug o' war with his caddie's arm had rattled him even more. He was in no mental state to recall the provisions of Rule 3-1b: 'A player may replace, with any club, a club which becomes unfit for play in the normal course of play.' In any case, would the humanitarian act of saving your caddie from a ducking constitute 'nor-

mal course of play'? Further, the clubs in the canal were temporarily inaccessible but perfectly fit for play.

Strange pegged up his ball and grabbed the two-iron. He found the fairway safely and now the green looked like a pocket handkerchief in the Sahara. If he found one of the bunkers he would be finished because he had no club left which was remotely suitable for an accurate explosion from sand. At moments like this those grinding hours on the practice ground pay off. Strange shortened his grip on the five-iron and hit a high, fading shot to the green. He did not exactly relish the putt but at least he now had the right club for the job and he made his vital four.

A diver recovered the lost clubs in time for the third round, except for the seven-iron which had sunk five feet into the soft silt and needed another day's probing with a rake before it eventually joined its fellows in Strange's bag.

An idol word

Bobby Jones was a superb writer, in addition to his accomplishments as a golfer, engineer and lawyer, and he is the best person to describe his own disaster:*

'Harry Vardon's first comment on my golf was at the National Open Championship in 1920, at Toledo, and I still regard it as the funniest and most conclusive estimate I ever heard on anything. By some happy circumstance, I was paired with Vardon, the Old Master, for the two qualifying rounds. I was delighted and more than a little flustered – Harry Vardon had been a hero and an idol to me ever since I first saw him play, when I was a kid 11 years old, at my home course in Atlanta.

'Harry and I were tied at the end of the first round at 76, I think, and in the second round I was doing a little better. We came to the seventh hole, a dogleg, with the drive over a yawning chasm and some tall trees, if the bold player would go straight for the green. Ted Ray really won the championship on this hole. It was a good par 4 and Ted got a 3 in each of the four rounds, being twice on the green with his drive, a punch of about 275 yards.

* from *Down the Fairway* (George Allen and Unwin).

'Harry and I took the big jump safely and were in front of the green, each with a short, plain little shot to get near the flag.

'Harry was a bit farther away and played a simple run-up, not far from the pin. In those days I loved to pitch, and elected to use a niblick, though there was no intervening trouble. I looked up on the shot and committed the most horrid mistake possible under the circumstances; I topped the ball and it scuttled like a rabbit straight over the green into a bunker. . . . To this day my ears get hot thinking of that shot.

'I played out for a bad 5, losing a stroke to par, and, desperately embarrassed, walked on to the next tee with Harry, who had not said a word thus far in the round. I thought I would ease my own embarrassment and break the ice at the same time. So I said:

'Mr Vardon, did you ever see a worse shot than that?'

He said: 'No.'

This appeared to close the incident.

Lead kindly miner's lamp

Life was good. The previous year Ben Crenshaw had won three tournaments and cleared more than quarter of a million dollars in prize money. Ever since his college days, Crenshaw had been tagged as a coming superstar and now those promises of a rich golfing destiny were coming true. Two days previously he had been hailed as a conquering hero once more as he won the Colonial Invitational. He was playing well, with not a care in the world and brimming with confidence. There was no reason that he could imagine why the good times should not go on and on. Even the weather was perfect, with not a breath of wind, as he pegged up his ball for the first round of the 1977 Memorial Tournament at Muirfield Village. Naturally, there was a huge gallery to watch the man of the moment.

The opening drive was not exactly flush off the middle of the clubface but it would do. Crenshaw had learnt to live with the odd stray drive. Nothing in his previous golfing experience, however, had prepared him for what followed. His clubs seemed possessed of an evil spirit: they had a mind of their own and a particularly malicious mind at that. Normally when a top-class tournament professional hits a shot off line he can repair any damage with a recovery shot. That is what golf is all about.

Nine times out of ten he can save his par, or better. On this occasion the stray shots flew unerringly into places which would have defied recovery with a three-inch mortar. 'On the 17th my ball was in such dense undergrowth that it was dark enough to need a miner's lamp,' he said later, when scar tissue had covered his wounded ego and he could speak rationally about his experience. When he finally completed the round he blushingly handed in his card for an 87.

A chair for Mr Miller

The year 1973 was to prove to be the ignition point of Johnny Miller's meteoric career with his victory in the US Open Championship, but it started badly. Since turning professional in 1969 he had been hailed as the coming superstar and sponsors had lavished endorsement contracts on him in the confident expectation of greatness.

Greatness was slow in embracing Miller. He had two minor tournament victories to show for nearly four years of hard campaigning and his frustration, and guilt towards those who had backed their faith in him, was sapping his morale and making him irritable.

His nerves, then, were tightly drawn in the Atlanta Open when he came to the last hole needing a par five for victory. The calculating, professional part of Miller's brain had no qualms about the hole, probably the best birdie chance on the Atlanta Country Club course. A steady drive followed by a four-iron, or maybe four-wood, would see him safely home. The human side of Miller's brain was in turmoil, with anticipation fighting impatience. However, the drive was adequate. Miller watched the ball boring directly towards the semi-rough on the right of the fairway and then, as hook-spin took effect, easing back onto course.

At this point Miller noticed a woman spectator sitting on a metal seat at about the spot where his ball would pitch. The woman also became aware of this possibility and she jumped up from the seat. Had she remained where she was, or had she moved the seat. . . . Well the story might have had a painful ending but Miller would surely have made five at the worst.

As it was a quirk of fate ordained that the ball should strike the metal seat at precisely the worst possible angle. Half an inch either way, even a quarter of an inch difference in the point of impact, would have saved the day for Miller.

As it was, the ball rebounded a hundred feet into the air, flying at an acute angle to the right. This freakish bounce deposited the ball four inches out of bounds and Miller's torment continued with increased virulence.

A self-respecting pro

Professional pride is strong on the American Tour. The players believe themselves to be the greatest exponents of golf in the world and if one player makes a hash of it they all feel diminished. At Harbour Town on Hilton Head Island Grier Jones looked up at the scoreboard and noticed with a shock that one of the competitors had posted a score of 86 for the Sea Pines Heritage Classic. In tones of righteous indignation he remarked: 'No self-respecting pro should ever shoot 86.'

His sentiments were natural and very possibly justified but this is one golf course where such indignation is best left unspoken. The next day a sweating and trembling Grier Jones spent an unconscionable time over a swinging eight-foot putt on the 18th green. Being a self-respecting pro he holed it – for an 85.

Fans are all very well, but . . .

As everyone knows, Jan Stephenson is more than a brilliant golfer. She is also a doll. Being a doll has its advantages, of course, but it is not all rich endorsement contracts and posing for glamorous pictures in the glossy magazines. There was a time when Jan discovered that being a doll was a definite hindrance to her golf career.

Year after year Jan dreaded playing in southern California because of a persistent side-effect of being a doll. It started with what she took to be a good-natured and flattering comment from behind the gallery ropes. 'Jan, I love you. Please, please marry me.'

For a professional golfer the crowd has to be an irrelevance to the job on hand, a threat to concentration and a presence to be ignored as far as possible. Most golf spectators are all too aware of their responsibilities and take care not to intrude on the consciousness of the players.

On this occasion Jan acknowledged the remark by smiling prettily and then settled over a putt, giving her full attention to considerations of line and length and pace. Her cocoon of concentration was shattered by a shout from the same voice. 'Sink this one and I'll give you the keys of a new Mercedes.'

Walking to the next tee Jan was confronted by her tormentor. He was, she judged, in his late thirties, dressed in the style known as Californian Classic – tight, tailored pants, shirt open almost to the waist to reveal clusters of gold chains, with hair carefully blow-dried to produce a look of casual neglect. He was on his knees, hands clasped, pleading: 'Marry me.'

Jan ignored him. 'At least favour me with a glance,' he wailed. On the next green he was at it again. 'Jan, I can help your putting if only you will marry me.' Golfers are normally philosophical about idiot spectators for the very good reason that if they make a fuss, or become involved in any kind of altercation, it is almost certain to put them off their game.

This creature was so importunate, however, that it was obvious that he represented a serious menace to the Australian girl's play, and police escorted him from the course. He was soon back. 'Jan darling. I promise never to hurt you again if you will just come back to me. I'm sorry. I'm sorry.'

The deranged fan tried to enlist the sympathy of other spectators by explaining that he and Jan had been secretly married for years. On one occasion in Los Angeles he repeated this confidence to a woman, not realizing that he was speaking to Jan's mother. She gave him a fierce verbal dressing-down, not that it dampened his ardour.

When the LPGA Tour moved east the lovelorn suitor pursued her by post. Jan was bombarded by poetry, if such a word can be applied to romantic outpourings written in golfing imagery on 12-foot scrolls, bordered with intricate designs.

The campaign reached its bizarre climax at San Diego in 1980. The pleading started early in the round and soon became so disruptive that, when the putting was completed on the fourth

green, the Pinkerton security men grabbed the Californian and marched him off to the parking area. He roared off in his tiny sports car in a state of frantic frustration.

As Jan lined up a 15-foot putt on the ninth her heart missed a beat as she heard the familiar plaintive voice. The words he was speaking sounded like gibberish to Jan, although she acknowledges that they may in fact have been Arabic. Nothing would surprise her about this guy. What was not to be doubted was that he was dressed in the flowing white robes and head-dress of an Arabian sheik, his imploring eyes screened behind dark sunglasses. Jan stabbed her putt wide of the hole and the Pinkertons moved in again, dragging the protesting sheik off to what Jan presumed was his camel or pink Rolls-Royce in the parking lot.

In recalling this incident Jan reflects that tournament golf is difficult enough when played in tranquil mood. Just how tough it was on this occasion when she was both excruciatingly embarrassed and spitting angry can be imagined. She was therefore relieved to reach the final green. But, no! There, standing against the ropes with arms folded in defiance stood an Indian chief in full regalia of buckskins, moccasins and massive head-dress of red and white feathers. The voice was unmistakable: 'Jan, I love you. If you make this putt I will marry you.'

The security men pounced. That was the end of the mystery stranger. Maybe the Pinkertons frightened him off. Maybe his ardour waned. Maybe it was all a cruel practical joke which wore too thin to sustain. Jan Stephenson's career went steeply into the ascendant.

'Up to now you haven't been trying.'

The entry of Mr and Mrs T. H. Cotton in the Calcot Scratch Foursomes naturally created considerable public interest and a large crowd gathered to watch them play. Toots, always a wilful woman and a doughty campaigner in the battle of the sexes, commanded that Henry play especially well so that her gallery would not be disappointed. She added: 'What's more, Cotton, don't you dare put me in the rough.'

Inevitably one of his drives ran through the fairway and finished in light semi-rough. To his horror Toots stomped up to the ball and whacked it straight back towards the tee. Most of the spectators were mystified and those who twigged were too well-bred to snigger but Henry's feelings can be imagined.

He thought he made a satisfactory riposte when he pulled out his brassie and hit the ball to within two feet of the flag. But Toots was not to be squelched like that. She holed the putt and addressed him tartly: 'That's the only way to treat you. Up to now you haven't been trying.'

And they won the tournament.

'Bad luck, George.'

The University of Maryland was playing Penn State and George Burns was in bad trouble when he shanked his second shot and watched in dismay as the ball soared over the perimeter fence, headed over a railway line and was clearly destined to finish in distant factory premises. Golf is a gentleman's game and its conventions demand expressions of sympathy for the misfortunes of an opponent. However, golfers are human and no vestige of blame can attach to the Penn State player if he experienced a purely reflex surge of gratitude at the unexpected gift of a hole even as he remarked sincerely: 'Bad luck, George.'

But wait. The powerfully struck ball hits a telephone wire. The wire stretches, just as the bow strings of the archers at Agincourt stretched to swing the fortunes of the battle. Under the inexorable laws propounded by Sir Isaac Newton, a telephone wire stretched under tension by a golf ball must in due course recoil. This it did, with a loud 'twang!', and the ball's direction was abruptly reversed from west to east. The kinetic energy imparted into the wire by the impact of the ball was just enough to propel the errant missile back to the green, where it rolled to an insouciant halt six feet from the hole.

The Penn State player collapsed in a heap. When he eventually regained a semblance of composure he entered into the surreal spirit of the incident by 12-putting.

Walter Mitty takes a crack at the Open

Once upon a time the championship committee of the Royal and Ancient golf club of St Andrews was made up of trusting men who took the world at face value. No trace of cynicism tainted their natures. In their own circle if a chap said he was eight-handicap a chap did not have to ask the chap to produce a handicap certificate because a chap's word was a sacred bond. Dammit, if a chap couldn't trust a chap then what would the world be coming to, eh?

Thus it came about that when an entry was received for the 1965 Open Championship from Walter Danecki of Milwaukee his name went straight into the draw for the qualifying rounds. After all the chap described himself as a professional golfer on the entry form, plain as day.

Danecki's appearance at Hillside caused no comment. He looked as much like a golfer as anyone else, a strapping six-footer of some forty-three summers. However, as soon as he swung a club it became obvious that Walter had not devoted too many of those summers to perfecting the arts of the royal and ancient game. He breezed around Hillside in a cool 108, a score which aroused the curiosity of the ever-alert golfing press.

Danecki explained that in fact he was a mail sorter 'but I wanted the crock of gold so my conscience made me write down "professional".' His golf credentials were, admittedly, meagre, consisting of seven years of occasional rounds over his local municipal course at $1.50 a time. The formalities for joining the PGA were too complicated and protracted and so he hit upon this idea of the British Open to cut through the red tape. 'What I will do is win one of the big ones and then they will have to let me in.' He added that he was self-taught, thought he could beat Arnold Palmer, and that he adhered to the spirit of the Professional Golfers' Association rules insofar as, not being a member, he did not charge for lessons.

The Royal and Ancient officials pondered the subject of Walter Danecki and came up with the statesmanlike solution which successive British governments had applied to most of the intractable problems of international affairs: ignore it and perhaps it will go away. They nominated a substitute to take Danecki's place in the second round, confident that he would lose no time in returning to Milwaukee.

Alas for their optimism, Danecki reported to the tee for his second round, eager to repair the damage of that opening 108. 'I don't like to quit. I like golf. That's what I came here to do.' He started, 7, 7, 8, and then, as the Americans say, the wheels came off and he scored 113, giving him a total which failed to qualify for the Open Championship by 75 strokes.

There is not, you might think, much that a golfer can say of a positive, heartening nature after such a performance. Walter was up to the challenge of the moment: 'I want to say that your small ball is right for this sort of course. If I had been playing our bigger ball I would have been all over the place.' All in all, he conceded, he was slightly discouraged by the events of these two days because, after all, he had been after the money.

This experience, as you may well imagine, alerted the R and A. Steps were taken to ensure that such an embarrassing fiasco could never happen again. Really? Eleven years later another entry from a professional escaped the scrutiny of the committee. Maurice Flitcroft, a 46-year-old crane driver from Barrow-in-Furness, had set his heart on winning the old claret jug and the fortune and glory which went with it. His apprenticeship for the qualifying ordeal was even sketchier than Danecki's for his association with the game was both brief and nominal. He had taken up golf 18 months previously and his experience was limited to hitting shots on the beach. When he was called to the tee at Formby for the first qualifying round he was embarking on the first 18 holes of his life.

On two holes his marker lost count of Maurice's earnest endeavours and gave him the benefit of the doubt, marking him for an 11 and a 12. The total came to 121 and Maurice put his finger squarely on the problem: 'At the start I was trying too hard. By the end of the round I felt that I was beginning to put it all together.' The evidence supported this diagnosis since his halves read 61, 60. This time the R and A was spared further embarrassment. Flitcroft withdrew from the competition with dignity: 'I have no chance of qualifying.' A reporter who went to the Flitcroft home that evening said to his mother: 'I have called about Maurice and the Open Championship.'

'Oh yes,' she replied with excitement. 'Has he won?'

Shanks and foozles in the press tent

By no means all golfing disasters are confined to golfers. Since tournaments are organized for the convenience of spectators and players, with no regard for newspaper edition times, the golf press probably represents the most disaster-prone body of men in the game. Most British Sunday papers, for instance, have an early edition for delivery in the remoter parts of Scotland and Ireland, and the last dot and comma has to be in the offices by five o'clock on Saturday afternoon.

It is quite astonishing how often the last putt in a tournament drops a few minutes before or after five p.m., and as the afternoon wears on the Sunday-paper writers tend to get a whit twitchy. There is no time for the well-polished phrase and the balanced cadence at this time, just a frantic scramble for the nearest telephone and a hurriedly ad-libbed 'top' to the story.

On the Saturday afternoon which scarred my soul for ever, nerves were drawn to concert pitch as Greg Norman putted out on the 18th green at Blairgowrie to record his first tournament victory in Europe.

Simultaneously the District Nurse, who had been in attendance in case of medical emergencies, decided nobody was going to break a leg standing around the last green and that she might as well make good her departure and beat the traffic. She climbed into her Morris Minor and drove sedately toward the exit. As she negotiated the corner of the press tent she was just a fraction over-meticulous in observing the highway code's injunction to keep to the left. Her rear fender snagged the telephone cable and hooked it cleanly, like a plane picking up an aircraft carrier's arresting wire, and off she drove quite oblivious to the fact that her car was dragging a skein of telephone cables behind her like a fork-load of spaghetti. The experience of the mass exit from the press tent of half-a-dozen demented writers, cursing like bargees and dashing to the car park for a Le Mans-style getaway in search of telephones, will haunt me for the rest of my days.

We returned individually, in vile ill-temper, hours later, for public telephone boxes in the Trossachs are few and far between. The old hands, inevitably, could cap this experience with even more horrific tales and I will confine myself to passing on just one of them, for it has a ludicrous quality about it which may give it a wider appeal than the usual newspaper 'shop'.

The year was 1948 and the occasion the final of the Amateur Championship at Royal St George's between Charlie Stowe and Frank Stranahan. In those days the Amateur was big news for this was still regarded as one of the world's major championships, one leg of the grand slam, and still basking in the lustre of Bobby Jones's magnificence.

The Press Association therefore made thorough preparations for coverage of the final. Two men were assigned and a private telephone was installed in a hut near the last green. If anything, the rivalry between the news agencies was even keener than it is today because the agency which got its stories onto the tapes first netted a considerable financial return. The two reporters planned their operation with stealth and cunning. It was unlikely that the match would finish on the home green so the senior writer, Graham Emery, worked out a rudimentary signalling system. He would follow play and dash to the top of the nearest sand dune the moment the winning putt dropped. If Stowe was the winner then Emery would semaphore with his umbrella, using vertical and horizontal movements to indicate the margin of victory. In the event of a Stranahan victory Emery would signal with his raised handkerchief, using the same code. The second reporter, Stan Lincoln, would have a line open to Press Association headquarters in London and he would scan the horizon through binoculars for the signal. He could then snap the result to a waiting world within seconds of the finish.

Lincoln was panning with his binoculars along the skyline when he heard the roar. Which, if any, of the myriad figures on the horizon was Emery? At that moment a sharp squall of rain swept across the links of St George's and five thousand umbrellas were raised on the instant.

The story really ought to end there. That is how a novelist would handle it, leaving the reader to imagine the recriminations from a frustrated sports editor burning the ears of poor Lincoln. The reader could well imagine Emery in a frenzy of frustration leaping up and down on his distant sand dune trying to elevate his signal above that forest of umbrellas, and that is exactly how it was. But your British golf writer is not without resource in an emergency and through his binoculars Lincoln picked up what appeared to be a disembodied handkerchief waving above the kaleidoscope of brightly coloured fabric. The rain obscured his vision but he concentrated hard and got the message. 'Stranahan won by 5 and 4' he yelled into the phone. True to the tradition of Julius Reuter and the doctrine that the news must get through at all costs, Emery had ripped up a stake used for gallery ropes and tied his handkerchief to it.

Is the barman a loose impediment?

There must be something about the air surrounding the 18th green at Moortown golf club, near Leeds. Down the years this area has earned a reputation as golf's Bermuda Triangle, the scene of numerous events which defy logical explanation. In the 1980 European Tournament Players' Championship, for instance, Severiano Ballesteros had a bare 120 yards to the flag for his approach shot. His ball lay sweetly on the close-cropped fairway turf and a good shot would give him the title.

By this stage of his career Ballesteros was no longer an excitable youth with adrenalin squirting from every pore at the prospect of winning a tournament. He was a battle-hardened champion and he took his time, checking the yardage and assessing the contours and condition of his target landing area. He selected his nine-iron and played a languid, three-quarters shot. The ball started off dead on line as it soared into the calm air of a summer's evening. It was still rising as it flew over the flagstick. On and on it flew, over the green, over the back fringe, over the horseshoe of grandstands behind the green. It pitched among the startled golfers who were improving the shining hour by honing their strokes on the practice putting green. Don't ask me how or why this freak shot happened. Above all, do not ask Ballesteros for he does not take kindly to intrusion into his private grief.

You might try asking the amateur, Nigel Denham, for he too was a victim of the Moortown Phenomenon and he might have a theory. In the 1974 English Amateur Strokeplay Championship he too was astonished to see his approach shot fly the green. The ball pitched on a pathway in front of the clubhouse, bounced up the steps through the open door, hit a wall and rebounded into the bar. Moments later the perplexed Denham followed, having

first been ordered to remove his golf shoes in accordance with the rules of the club. He found his ball sitting on the carpet and surrounded by members in whom alcoholic refreshment had released unsuspected talents for ribald remarks.

Denham consulted the local rules and confirmed that the clubhouse was not out of bounds. It followed that his ball lay within an obstruction from which no relief was available. He could move a chair or a table but, having done so, there was no interference with his stance or the intended area of his swing. Therefore, he reasoned, he must play the ball as it lay. He had 20 yards to the green and, to facilitate the shot, he opened the window. He played a crisp shot through the open window and the ball finished 12 feet from the hole, to a resounding ovation from the drinkers.

In the fullness of time the details of this daring stroke were conveyed to the Rules of Golf Committee at St Andrews for adjudication. The committee ruled that Denham should have been penalized two strokes for opening the window. Chairs, tables, beer mats and sundry impediments could be cleared aside with impunity as movable obstructions but the window, as an integral part of the immovable obstruction of a clubhouse, should not have been moved.

Meanwhile the committee of Moortown pondered the incident and declared the clubhouse out of bounds.

Savaged by a pigeon

Bo Wininger did not make much of a splash as a tournament professional, although he had been a useful amateur, but he moved up into a different class when he was playing for a fat pot in a private match. The word 'hustler' is sometimes used to convey connotations of sharp practice, but I use it in its pure and totally honourable sense of a golfing gambler. Lee Trevino became a great player because of his long apprenticeship as a hustler, ready to play anybody, any time, for any stake.

The week before the New Orleans Open Wininger was in Oklahoma where he had the good fortune to meet a sportsman with a fast backswing and an expansive attitude to money. They had a tight and exciting match, thanks to Wininger's generosity in the matter of allowing his opponent rather more handicap strokes than he was strictly due. As happens with such uncanny frequency in these encounters, the professional scraped home on the last green and soon the two of them were in the bar, with Wininger drying the ink on a cheque for $5000 by flapping it idly in the air while trying not to look smug.

'The only problem now,' he remarked, 'is how to get myself to New Orleans.'

'That's no problem,' said the sportsman, 'you can take my car.'

'But how could I get it back to you?' asked Wininger.

'Oh, you're bound to run into somebody down there who will be only too happy to drive it back here,' said the sportsman.

The first rule of the hustler is that when you run into a lucky streak you ride it all the way. Thus Wininger found himself driving south in a new Cadillac and congratulating himself on a satisfactory day's work.

At this period there were still rural communities whose main source of income was in gouging dollar bills from transients driving through in Cadillacs. Wininger was stopped, led to the slammer, fingerprinted and documented and relieved of as much of his worldly wealth as the officer felt was commensurate with the offence of speeding.

Wininger accepted that his lucky streak had run out and went on his way. As he ran into the outskirts of New Orleans he was stopped again by a patrol car. The occupants seemed to have been lying in wait for him.

'Is this your vehicle, buddy?'

'It's on loan, I am driving it with the permission of the owner.'

'Oh yeah?' The officer checked the plates and the engine number. 'No doubt about it. You want to come with us?'

For the second time that day Wininger found himself behind bars. He was mystified. Perhaps word had gone out on the police grapevine that he was an easy touch.

When the questioning began Wininger found it difficult, nay impossible, to establish his innocence. It became clear that the New Orleans police had received a report of a stolen car. It was also established beyond a peradventure that the Cadillac was that stolen car. The question exercising Wininger was whether his opponent had stolen the car or whether he had reported it stolen as revenge for being relieved of $5000. His discomfiture was compounded by the fact that the hot car report had been followed by a second report, accompanied by a full description and fingerprints, of the man caught speeding away from the city where the car had been stolen.

The story about being lent the car by a complete stranger, with no provision having been made for its return, did not greatly impress the New Orleans constabulary. As corroboration Wininger produced the cheque. The police quickly established it as a clumsy forgery. The Cadillac's owner had carelessly left his cheque-book in the glove compartment of the car.

It was several hours before Wininger was able to register his entry at the golf club for the New Orleans Open. He did not play very well that week.

On reflection, a bad idea

Anyone who spends some time around golf tournaments gets used to a curious habit of professional golfers. At odd moments, such as waiting at bus stops, or during lulls in play, the dedicated professional will take a club from his bag, swing it slowly back and then freeze. At this point he turns his head and squints along the line of his extended left arm.

To the uninitiated it might seem that he must be checking whether the clubhead is still attached to the shaft or, possibly, whether his hand is attached to his wrist. Both these conditions are essential prerequisites for golf but reassurance may be obtained without making a half-swing. What the pro is actually doing is checking the alignment of his left wrist and the position of the clubhead. The idea is that if these things are right at the bus stop, or in the locker room, then there is a good chance that they will be right in the heat of battle on the golf course. If they are wrong, however, then remedial measures can be put in hand.

There is nothing like a full-length mirror to stimulate a golfer into this ritual. With a mirror there are many other desirable points available for scrutiny and critical analysis. The pro can check the angle of his shoulders, the inward tilt of the left knee, the bracing of the left side of his torso and the set of his Dick Tracy jaw-line.

The hallway of the Marriott hotel in Ardmore, Philadelphia, is lined with mirrors and the opportunity was irresistible to

Terry Diehl on the eve of the US Open Championship of 1980. Out came a club and in a trice Diehl was swinging it back. A milli-trice later there was a tinkling of breaking glass and an uttering of muted oaths. An ornate light fitting was shattered and the first knuckle of Diehl's left pinkie was gushing blood. The wound required eight stitches and Diehl scored 144 round Merion in his first two rounds, roughly one stroke for each pain-killing tablet he consumed.

Putting mixtures, moderation and excess

There is a long and more or less honourable tradition in amateur golf for a snort of putting mixture to steady the nerves before venturing onto the golf course. Kummel was claimed to have remarkable soothing qualities on the palsy which accompanies the day's first five-foot putt. Doctors have long warned that the caffeine in the breakfast cup of coffee has a deleterious effect on the sense of balance, and conscientious golfers have sought to suppress this reaction by stunning the caffeine with a slug of cognac.

However, the benefits of alcohol do not increase in proportion to the dosage and occasionally golfers fail to appreciate that curious inverse logic. After all, it is a perfectly natural mistake to assume that if one is good then two must be better.

At one period of his career the brilliant Canadian stylist, George Knudson, had a little difficulty in judging the optimum quantity and the best timing of the medication. He habitually wore tinted glasses, but the brilliant sunshine, multiplied by reflection from the Nevada desert, struck him with shattering force as he stepped out of the clubhouse for the first round of the Sahara Invitational tournament.

He pegged his ball on the first tee, took his driver and looked down the fairway towards the rising sun which was just working up to maximum wattage. He closed his eyes and then directed his uncertain gaze at the turf. His ball looked to be the size of a grapefruit and also to be on fire, shimmering with a brilliance which bored into his head like the arc-light of a welding torch. He tried another tenative glance down the fairway. He came to a decision. He bent down, picked up the ball and the tee peg and delivered the line which has become legendary in the game: 'Call the first alternate.'

Marvin 'Bud' Ward was another victim of failing to observe the cardinal rule of putting mixtures. After two rounds of the 1949 US Open Championship at Medinah, Ward was not far off the lead. In those days the final two rounds were played on the same day and Ward understood all too well that he faced a daunting mental challenge and a long physical ordeal. It would, therefore, be no less than prudent to get a sustaining snort under his belt, especially as it would give him a definite edge over his two main rivals, the teetotal Sam Snead and the man whose professional ethics would never permit him to be seen in the bar at breakfast time, Dr Cary Middlecoff.

As the barman was filling Ward's prescription, a friend chanced by, bent on a similar mission. 'What can I offer you?' asked Ward with old-world courtesy. In due course convention demanded that the friend reciprocate Ward's hospitality. Another friend joined them. Ward never made it to the first tee.

A jug of black coffee

One of the drawbacks, or advantages if you prefer, of being an Irish golfer is that pretty well everywhere you go in the world there is an Irish colony or a seminary, which comes to the same thing. In short, there are always pressing invitations for a jar and a bit of crack. Let us label that fact Circumstance A.

The World Cup was founded to generate international good-will through golf. Friendship and conviviality are therefore supposed to be essential ingredients of the tournament and Christy O'Connor has a powerful talent for friendship and conviviality. Indeed, many good judges are convinced that O'Connor's genius for hitting a golf ball would have won him several Open Championships if only nature had endowed him less liberally with the conviviality. As to that, I hesitate to express an opinion. All I know is that he is a man in a million and among the finest strikers of a golf ball I have ever seen. Shall we for convenience refer to O'Connor's loyalty to the essential purpose of the World Cup as Circumstance B?

At the 1963 World Cup at St Nom la Breteche, near Paris, Circumstance A and Circumstance B combined to produce Circumstance C, namely that the golf correspondent of the *Daily Express*, Mark Wilson, went into the locker-room five minutes before the Irish team was due to hit off and there discovered O'Connor. He was seated, holding his head in his hands in the hope of preventing it from exploding, and moaning.

'You're due on the tee,' said Wilson.

'Coffee,' said Christy.

'You'll be called any minute now.'

'Black,' said Christy.

'There is no time for coffee.'

'Black coffee,' said Christy.

'You haven't even got your shoes on.'

'A big jug of black coffee,' said Christy, experimentally opening one eye.

'I can't bring you coffee on the first tee. There's thousands of people out there.'

O'Connor heaved himself slowly to his feet, lurched sideways in an easterly direction and then on a westerly vector before settling in the upright mode.

'You know the first hole?' inquired Christy.

Wilson nodded. *Daily Express* golf correspondents are generally well informed on the location of the first hole.

'There is a 200-yard post on the side of the fairway.'

'Yes,' said Wilson.

'It's about 200 yards from the tee,' added Christy helpfully.

'Right,' said Wilson.

'Pace off 65 yards from that post,' said Christy, vainly trying to stuff his right foot into his left shoe.

'Check,' said Wilson.

'Wait in the woods for me,' said Christy.

'I will, I will,' said Wilson.

'With the coffee, you bollux,' said Christy.

'With the coffee,' confirmed Wilson.

'Black,' said Christy, triumphantly solving the mysterious permutation of feet and shoes.

'Black coffee,' said Wilson, departing in the direction of the cafeteria.

Wilson followed his instructions to the letter, stationing himself in the woods with a steaming jug of black coffee. A golf ball clattered among the branches above him and fell nearby. In due course it was followed by O'Connor, walking with the uneasy gait of a man whose central nervous system has lost its lines of communication to the further outposts of the empire.

The crowds around the first tee had maintained an embarrassed silence at O'Connor's opening drive. Little did they appreciate that they had just witnessed one of the greatest golf shots of all time.

O'Connor swallowed the coffee at a draught and marched on, a giant refreshed. It was not one of his more memorable rounds but three under par was a respectable score. Under those three Circumstances.

A new angle on the professional golfer

The professional golfer does not live by golf alone. As a public figure who parades before the populace at tournaments, and before an even greater multitude on television, he has a value to the fashion industry. In short, golfers are paid to wear different brands of clothing. In theory this is a mutually satisfactory arrangement. In practice, fashion designers are not always sympathetic to the special requirements of golfers. It is clear that the designers have a vision of what man should be, a tapering isosceles triangle. Clothing is thus designed to accommodate such an ideal. But golfers, as we can all observe, come in different shapes and sizes. There are oblongs and rectangles and ovoids whom nature never intended for the triangular look.

Likewise, the designers overlook the fact that those golfers who do not conform to the geometry of Michelangelo and Leonardo da Vinci are required to do more than hold a statuesque pose. They have to move about and bend, particularly bend. It therefore happens fairly frequently that embarrassment overtakes contemporary sportsmen who appear on the first tee in tight-fitting magenta trousers.

The act of teeing up a ball, or retrieving one from the hole, puts an intolerable strain on the seams. In the majority of cases the player hears the sundering if he does not feel the draught and immediately covers his embarrassment by slipping on his rain trousers. But every now and again the mishap goes unnoticed by all except the twenty thousand spectators and the ten million television viewers. In such cases the shame when the victim detects the cause of the mass sniggering from behind the gallery ropes is quite excruciating.

Baldovino Dassu, for example, was puzzled by the levity of the crowd at the Swiss Open. The young Italian World Cup player could have understood, if not forgiven, some expressions of amusement if he had been playing badly. But on this occasion he was inspired and was taking apart the Alpine course at Crans-sur-Sierre.

He finished with a European Tour record of 60 and was brought into the press room for interview. The ribald golfing press quickly revealed all, namely that every time he bent down *he* had revealed all. His trousers were split clear up to the waistband.

Graham Marsh won the Japanese Pepsi-Cola tournament in 1981 and the popular Australian was invited to give a television interview on the first tee. He duly obliged, speaking fluently and modestly in reply to the interviewer's questions despite some frantic and incomprehensible gestures from behind the camera. Marsh assumed that this pantomime was some form of television code from director to interviewer, possibly a signal to speed up the proceedings, and he continued unabashed with his peroration.

On completion of this chore he asked the director, 'Was that all right?'

'No, Mr Marsh,' said the distraught director, 'your fly was undone.'

Thish ish the shixteensh . . .

A television performer needs dramatic talent, a presence, a voice, self-assurance and the right appearance in addition to specialized knowledge of his subject. For CBS golf commentator, Ben Wright, all those attributes vanished in the twinkling of an eye at four o'clock in the morning before the third round of the 1978 Western Open.

Wright had spent a convivial evening before retiring to his room, resulting in a nocturnal visit to the bathroom. He was suffering from a dry cough at this time and it was a chesty spasm which dislodged his upper bridge. Wright's desperate lunge to retrieve his expensive dental accessories was a fraction too slow and the gleaming ingredients of his winning smile were flushed into oblivion as his fingers groped feverishly in the swirling waters.

Things always seem worse at four o'clock in the morning and Wright was terrified that his television career was finished. The director would have to replace him for that afternoon's telecast; the substitute commentator would have a huge success and he would be offered a permanent contract in place of the unreliable and accident-prone Wright. Frank Chirkinian, the amiable Armenian who masterminds CBS golf, would surely conclude that the accident was the result of a drunken binge. In the event, Wright was correct in that assumption, anyway.

He telephoned the hotel maintenance man, his feverish imagination grasping for the only straw it could conceive. Was there perhaps a sump, or filter, in the hotel's drainage system and, if so, would the maintenance man be so kind as to dash down there and probe for the absent teeth?

The recipient of this call was less than ecstatic at this suggestion. For a start, he had the greatest difficulty in understanding the hysterical caller, what with the unfamiliar English vowel sounds and the fact that the words were distorted by a whistling lisp. When he eventually accepted that he was not the victim of a drunken practical joke, and he comprehended the bizarre request being made on his professional services, the honest Mid-Westerner was aghast. He would not be a party to such an enterprise. Even if there was some way of intercepting the teeth, which there wasn't, he would not be an accomplice in an enterprise which projected the vile possibility of the teeth being restored to a human mouth.

Wright gloomily surveyed himself in the bathroom mirror. With only his two front teeth left in place he looked like a distraught Bugs Bunny. His voice sounded like a steam whistle in the terminal stages of disrepair. It was a very dispirited Ben Wright who reported to the CBS compound at the golf club. Chirkinian was merciless: 'You will just have to talk tight-lipped.'

Wright asked around the complex whether anyone happened to have a dental appointment for that morning. By chance an assistant director had made an appointment to repair a loose filling and agreed that Wright's problem was more critical. Thus it came about that Wright found himself in the surgery of Dr Fu.

'You have ploblem?'

'Yeshshsh,' said Wright in a poor imitation of a deflating whoopee cushion.

Dr Fu proved to be a friend indeed. He cancelled his other engagements and went to work and in the space of four hours created a replacement bridge which fitted perfectly.

Wright's collapsed face was restored to its customary fullness and his voice returned to normal. He went back to the golf club in time for rehearsal and taping of those familiar introductions: 'I'm Ben Wright and I will be describing the play on this challenging 17th hole.'

That was not quite the end of the incident. Television crews are notorious for their malicious sense of fun and even at the best of times they go to extreme lengths to shatter the composure of the performers. Word of Wright's predicament had got around and so it came about that during the run-through of the pre-taped material, when it came to the point where Wright did his opening introduction to camera, there on the monitor was a picture of the 17th green. In what is known in the business as a tight two-shot, there was the flagstick and a set of clockwork false teeth on the turf. In perfect synchronization with the clattering choppers was the recorded voice of Wright: 'I'm Ben Wright and I will be describing . . . .'

That piece of film is still in the archives of the CBS black museum which contains all the material felt to be unsuitable for public showing.

Till death or disqualification do us part . . .

These days John Laupheimer is the Commissioner of the Ladies' Professional Golf Association but the episode which sent painful shock waves in all directions occurred at the time when he was a senior administrator of the US Golf Association. He was a referee at the CPC Women's International and was watching when the stalwart of the British Curtis Cup team, Mary Everard, was requested by her playing companion, Julia Greenhalgh, to mark and lift her ball.

Both were just through the back of the fourth green and

Mary's ball lay on the line of Julia's shot. Mary accordingly marked her ball, lifted it and handed it to her caddie. To Laupheimer's horror the caddie proceeded to clean the ball, an infringement of Rule 23-2 carrying a penalty of one stroke.

Laupheimer is a man of highest principle, administering the rules without fear or favour. He it was who had to disqualify Severiano Ballesteros for being late on the tee in the 1980 US Open Championship and on this occasion he did not hestitate to perform his painful duty. As Mary walked to the next tee he informed her of this infraction of the rules. Mary was livid with rage. Nothing he could say would calm her anger. There was no point in Laupheimer explaining that he was actually doing her a favour, since unless she had included that penalty stroke on her card someone might have reported the infraction to the committee and she would be disqualified.

A favour indeed! Mary refused to listen to a word, or to utter a word in reply to this reptilian busybody with his witch-hunting rule book and sanctimonious talk about it all being for her own good. It was another five holes before Mary could bring herself to exchange a chilly word or two with the wretch.

The third player in this group was Alice Dye, wife of Pete Dye, the celebrated golf-course architect. She related the incident on the telephone to her husband and next day on the practice ground she called Laupheimer over to pass on Pete's response: 'John knows a lot about the rules of golf but he doesn't know much about being married.'

Oh, didn't I mention that Everard was Mary's maiden name? She and John Laupheimer had been married less than six months previously.

Rommel makes his deadline

Jack Statter was a genius, of that there is no doubt. The form of his genius is difficult to define because his special talent was simply for living. Nobody I ever met got more out of life or put more into it, and if he became bored with the life of Jack Statter then he lived somebody else's life for a bit. It could be slightly disconcerting to be with him during the transition. One minute you would be talking to Jack Statter about his family, say, and his voice would crack with emotion as he recalled how awful it had been for his son when the generals came to take him away. I enjoyed those sessions with Field-Marshal Irvin Rommel but I found Lawrence of Arabia slightly austere as a drinking companion and Captain Horatio Hornblower became tiresomely truculent in his cups. The day he discovered a sign in a Dublin shop reading 'Ears pierced while you wait' Jack was so elated that he became Sean O'Casey and started to write a play about golf correspondents called *Juno and the Pay-phone.*

By profession Jack was a stone sub, a journalist who works in the composing room and performs all the last-minute editorial tasks needed to get the paper out on time. He was a brilliant technician and his finest hour was when the critical deadline arrived one night and there was not enough printed type to fill the page. Jack's solution was to have the printer set in bold type:

There's
more
news
in
the
SUN

The slogan filled the space perfectly and the page went on time. Jack so relished the irony of this stratagem that he had blocks made of the slogan in different shapes and sizes. When a waspish mood was upon him he would throw a news item out of a page to accommodate one of his blocks.

In the summer months the *Sun* used Jack as golf correspondent and since the newspaper was interested only in sensational events, Jack largely ignored the golf and sought the human interest stories among the caddies and spectators.

It was such a quest which brought him to the ambulance which was in attendance for a tournament in Wales. In order to avoid distress or embarrassment to those involved, I will not specify the time and place precisely. Jack's magnetic personality immediately enslaved the duty nurse and before long the ambulance was ringing with merry laughter. Since the nurse could not leave her post to accompany Jack to the bar, his usual research headquarters, out came the medicinal brandy, with which the ambulance was liberally supplied. The merriment increased throughout the day which, fortunately, produced no medical emergencies.

By six o'clock in the evening the only part of Jack's brain which was not thoroughly marinated in brandy was the lobe or nodule which controls professional responsibility. Since darkness was falling it must be time to dictate his report to the office. He staggered into the press tent and, operating by reflex, successfully managed to dial the right number. It now dawned on him that he did not have a report to dictate. Frantically he went through his pockets. Out came a crumpled sheet of paper and Jack scanned it with amazement. A miracle. There, in his sprawling handwriting, was an excellent story, succinctly told.

Enunciating each word with extreme clarity, Jack Statter dictated his report of the previous day. And the *Sun* printed it.

Faith, hope and clarity

Success at golf depends as much, if not more, on self-belief and confidence as it does on prowess. It is in this vital department of faith that the support of a loyal wife can make a vast contribution to a golfer's career. The contribution made to golf by Barbara Nicklaus and Winnie Palmer is immeasurable but undoubted, and freely acknowledged as such by their husbands.

During the Atlanta Classic of 1980 Mrs Kathy Shearer telephoned the golf club and the following conversation ensued:

'Could you please tell me what Bob Shearer shot?'

'63 Ma'am.'

'No, Shearer. That's S - H - E - A - R - E - R.'

5

All God's creatures

O judgement! thou art fled to brutish beasts,
And men have lost their reason.

William Shakespeare, *Julius Caesar*

The things you see when you haven't got a gun

Intervention by animals is often doubly infuriating because of its shock value. There is a strong strain of W. C. Fields in every golfer's attitude to children. We recognize their potential for mischief and when we see a small boy loitering just off the fairway at driving distance we are subconsciously braced for villainy.

If the pestilential delinquent snatches up the ball, hops over a fence and makes good his escape on his waiting getaway bicycle, as happened to Christy O'Connor Junior in a tournament at Bournemouth, then we do at least have the satisfaction of having our prejudices confirmed. As we rant and curse, we can reflect on how right we were to regard snotty-nosed kids as natural enemies.

But if, as frequently happens, a bird flies off with a ball the act of larceny is compounded by sheer betrayal. We have always been fond of birds. Dammit, the wife even puts out scraps of bread for the robins in winter. We have never in our lives entertained a malicious thought against the black-backed gull and the act thereby looms as doubly dastardly.

Even worse is the reaction of our fellow golfers. If a boy commits an act of hooliganism on a golf course, then the adult world of golf closes ranks and in the true spirit of solidarity fires a massive salvo of verbal abuse across the generation gap.

You don't get far if you try to muster support for an armed posse to blast every black-backed gull out of the sky. Your playing companions are more likely to be rolling about in helpless laughter at your misfortune.

At Purley Downs golf club, south of London, the first hole is a par three steeply downhill to a saucer set in a clearing of the wooded valley. For years a wise old dog fox lurked in the woods and when it heard a ball smack into the inviting turf of the green, it trotted slowly from its hiding place, picked up the ball in its teeth and trotted slowly back into the woods. It scorned shots which missed the green and thereby vastly increased its capacity for inducing apoplexy on the tee. One of the most delicious feelings to be experienced in golf is to hit one close to the flag with the opposition safely plugged in a bunker. So life within Purley Downs golf club was enlivened by a succession of puce-faced members seeking support for a motion that the fox be hounded, snared, shot, trapped, poisoned, gassed or zapped by aerial bombardment. The pro-fox faction always carried the day by a comfortable majority.

Apart from the unconventional hobby of shooting sharks with an army rifle off the coast of his native Australia, Greg Norman shares this humane attitude towards the animal kingdom. At the 1982 European Open at Sunningdale, Norman was going well and looking a likely winner of the valuable first prize when he pegged up his ball on the seventh tee. Norman loves driving. It is his favourite shot and a money-winner, for he is the longest straight driver in the world. He had to get the ball airborne quickly because the land rises sharply ahead of this tee to an unseen fairway over the brow. That presented no problem to the accomplished Norman. He set his powerful frame into the address position and wound up for another mighty drive.

As he was starting down, and past the point where he could stem the accumulating surge of power, a worm broke the surface an inch behind the ball. Norman's instinctive reflexes caused him to pull up on the club to prevent decapitating the creature's waving extremity. As a consequence the clubhead met the ball in the region of the equator and you know the result when this happens. The ball departed with its usual velocity approaching 200 miles an hour but on a flight path about an inch above the surface of the tee.

The ball plugged deeply into the embankment about 25 yards ahead of Norman and its extrication was complicated by the luxuriant growth of heather around the crater. To his credit, Norman refrained from seeking vengeance on the worm, which retreated to subterranean safety, but that untimely blind interloper removed at least one digit from the sum on his pay cheque that week.

Ants in the pants and elsewhere

The ant is not classified as a burrowing animal under the provisions of Rule 32. The ant, by implication, is a creature of no consequence, a mere insect and, as such, unworthy of recognition by the lordly legislators of the Rules of Golf Committee. That is understandable: in 500 years no golfer has been seriously inconvenienced by the cast made by a burrowing ant on the Old Course at St Andrews. The same is not true of equatorial Africa. Here ants' nests rise as 20-foot stalagmites, hard as brick and often with trees or shrubs growing from their summits. In Africa the cast made by burrowing ants creates interferences as severe as Nelson's Column, circumstantial evidence that the creatures which built it are no ordinary ants.

Jack Newton could not believe that the mighty columns on Ndola golf course were built by ants. The locals were pulling his leg. Newton was doing well in the Cock o' the North tournament and had no time for distracting thoughts of ants. His second shot to the 17th had finished to the right of the green and as Newton was contemplating the lie of his ball his caddie dropped the bag, shouted: 'Ants, bwana!' and fled for his life. The astonished Newton stood rooted to the spot. 'What the . . .?' At this point he became sharply uprooted as a hundred pins jabbed hard into various parts of his body. He danced, yelling rich Australian oaths and slapping at his body. The African ant is virtually crush-proof as well as being possessed of mandibles which can chew mahogany as easily as you and I bite through marshmallow. They can reduce an elephant to a heap of white bones and Newton was clearly proving to be delicious.

There was, as he quickly realized, only one way to save his bacon. More ants were arriving by the hundred and, unless he acted without delay, they would soon be retiring to their fortress, belching quietly, asking each other if there were any toothpicks about and leaving his skeleton by the green.

He tore off his clothes. All of them. Particularly all of them. This was no time for the modest retention of his underpants because one brigade of this monstrous regiment clearly had

specialized tastes. His wife Jackie joined in the counter-attack, doing her best to shield her husband from the amused public gaze while desperately safeguarding her wifely vested interest from further depredations.

A trained athlete whose posterior is being injected with formic acid can move faster than an ant, and that helped. The Newtons moved to ant-free territory, with both of them picking off the survivors and flaying his legs and back with his discarded clothing.

The next day Newton was indulging in one of his favourite pastimes, casting an appraising eye over the female spectators or, in the inelegant phrase of pro golf, clocking the grumble. Alongside the fifth fairway he spotted a gorgeous girl and, in the manner of healthy males, he started mentally to undress her. Talk about the wish being father to the thought. At that very moment the girl started slapping herself frantically. Newton smiled, for he knew what must happen next. And it did.

Jack Newton won the tournament.

Course wild life

(i) Rabbits

The rabbit gets a pretty sweet deal from the human race. True, farmers are not ecstatic about having their crops nibbled and tend to zap the furry little creatures with shotguns, but the rest of us, by and large, are pro-rabbit. That is understandable when you consider the conditioning we receive from rabbit propagandists. It starts in the cradle where babies are dressed in rabbit suits and the image-making continues remorselessly at every stage of childhood. Bunny rabbit motifs on nursery furniture prepare the young minds for the brain-washing stories of Enid Blyton and then the advanced mind-bending of Lewis Carrol's White Rabbit, not to mention a constant bombardment of cartoon rabbits on television. We grow up with a glowing, sentimental regard for rabbits and this emotion is powerful enough to soften even the stony hearts of members of the Rules of Golf Committee.

What do you imagine lies behind Rule 32? You surely do not think that you get a free drop from the casts made by burrowing animals because the committee felt the game should be made easier for golfers? No, no. The rule is there to protect the lovable, cuddly, fun-loving rabbits which never did anybody the slightest harm. If it were not for that rule every golfer in the land would demand that the green committee get out there with poison gas, snares, ferrets, flamethrowers and hand grenades to exterminate every one of those smelly, verminous, buck-toothed pests. Rule 32 allows golfers and rabbits to co-exist and it preserves the warm special relationship between the two species. Except in the case of Miss Jennie Lee Smith.

Miss Lee Smith was converted from pro-rabbit to anti-rabbit during the fourth round of the British Women's Open Championship at Gosforth Park.

On the 10th hole she scored eight, which was not like the player who was to become Britain's most successful woman professional, but it happened. She was, therefore, not at peak morale as she teed her ball to play the short 11th. These things rankle. Golfers are supposed to shrug off disappointments and devote their full concentration to the next shot but that is sometimes easier said than done. Her tee shot, not to beat about the bush, was a shank, and the ball squirted away right in the sickening way that shanked shots have, to finish wide of the green in beating-about-the-bush country.

Miss Lee Smith was therefore not at her most resilient as she advanced with pitching wedge at the ready. At least she could see her ball, nestling among tuffety grass. She assessed the shot and then proceeded to take up her stance, first the left foot and then. . . . She was transfixed with terror. The volume was shattering but what really terrified her was the human quality of that shriek of pain. She had plonked her spiked shoe down on a baby rabbit cowering under a tuffet.

In fact the rabbit was not badly hurt and scurried off but Miss Lee Smith was destroyed. Shaking from shock, her nerves totally destroyed, she could not wait to finish the round and reach the rabbit-free safety of the clubhouse. At last it was over and she reached with relish for the glass of cool lager which would ease the dry constrictions in her throat. Unnoticed on the far rim of the glass a wasp took violent exception to being tilted skywards. It stung her on the nose.

(ii) Bees

Every golfer has a sting story although it is doubtful if there was ever a sting quite so significant as the one which very possibly cost the United States the World Cup of 1982. The victim was Calvin Peete and the sting was bad enough to cause him to withdraw from the American team. Since this happened at a time when he had just established himself as the most formidable golfer in America, the bee which did the damage was due a vote of thanks from Manuel Pinero and José Maria Canizares, who won the Cup for Spain.

Gary Player and Jack Nicklaus prudently avoided a disaster during an exhibition match at Zwartkop, South Africa, in 1966 when they were attacked by a swarm of wild bees. They covered their heads with towels and ran for it, settling for a half on the bee-infested hole without striking a shot. If that sounds slightly timorous of them, running away from a few insects, it should be realized that African wild bees are the most lethal form of wildlife in the sub-continent, killing more people each year than poisonous snakes or big game.

(iii) Ostriches

On a goodwill tour of South America with Jimmy Demaret, Sam Snead was setting himself to play a bunker shot when Demaret said: 'Look behind you.' Snead turned and was confronted by an ostrich bearing down on him with beak open and ready for action. The bird was, in fact, a pet of the golf club and its innocent intention was merely to eat Snead's straw hat. He knew nothing of all that, of course, and automatically raised his arm to protect himself. The ostrich, for its part, knew nothing of Snead's intentions and naturally clamped its beak on his hand. It was two weeks before Snead's hand was sufficiently healed for him to play golf properly again.

(iv) Grouse

It should be added that all this mayhem caused to golfers by the animal kingdom is by no means a one-way traffic. Golfers have taken a fearful toll of birds and beasts with their flashing clubs and flying golf balls, and even fish have not been immune from aerial bombardment with fatal consequences.

The saddest case I can discover occurred in Scotland on 12 August 1975. Need I draw special attention to the significance of that date? The Glorious Twelfth of August is the day upon which the law permits grouse to be shot and the start of the shooting season is always marked by a concerted onslaught on the small bird which is specially bred and cosseted by a humane society for the purpose of being blown to pieces. Now birds are not quite so daft as they might sometimes appear. That expression 'bird-brained' may be a foul calumny because there is plenty of evidence to prove that grouse learn a bit about shooting. They get to know the places where they are safe and a golf course is an obvious sanctuary from the guns.

I like to think of one particular grouse being alerted by the sound of gunfire and deciding to high-tail it pronto to the safety of Kingussie golf course. It jinks and swerves to avoid the menace of swinging double-barrels and breathes a hugh sigh of relief as it flashes over the perimeter fence of Kingussie. I've made it, home and free. Whew! That was a close one. Then POW! A golf ball struck from the tee by Willie Fraser, aged 11, hits the grouse and kills it instantly.

Serpentine events in the desert

The United States Golf Association does not represent itself to be a particularly benevolent body but its heart is in the right place and it is surely pure compassion which guides its policy of withholding the names of disgruntled golfers who appeal for justice to the Rules of Golf Committee.

Most of the appellants are, as becomes obvious from their pompous, self-important complaints, prime candidates to be put in the stocks and pelted with rotten eggs. However, in handing down their Decisions the wise men of the Rules of Golf Committee conceal the identities of these litigants under the sobriquets of Player A and Player B.

It may be that I am being harsh and traducing the characters of quite respectable people who write to the committee and that they are honest and respectable folk who are simply seeking enlightenment on knotty points of law. However, to one who chooses the consolidated Decisions as his favourite bedtime reading, having outgrown the insipid Marquis de Sade, it is inevitable that the Player A who wants his opponent horse-whipped for using a tee peg as a ball marker should eventually loom in the reader's mind as the same Player A who is raising nit-picking points in all the other Decisions.

Thus my hatred and contempt tends to focus on a select coterie of alphabetical figures, personified in one particular harpy whose place in the annals of infamy can be designated only by the pseudonym of Player B. According to the deposition of Player A we may deduce that the bestial behaviour of Player B took place on a course in Arizona, or possibly New Mexico.

At all events they were engaged in a match and Player A had the misfortune to hit an approach shot into a bunker alongside a green. To her dismay she saw that the ball had come to rest hard by the chilling coils of a sleeping rattlesnake.

You never know with rattlesnakes. Probably, reasoned Player A, they are light sleepers. Almost certainly, she further conjectured, they are prone to the common condition of being a bit testy on first waking. The likelihood of such testiness would surely be increased if the cause of the waking was a sharp belt in the ribs from a sand-wedge on the follow-through of an explosion shot. Even a sweet-natured rattlesnake would be liable to react to such an interruption to its slumbers. Player A threw herself on the charity and the milk of human kindness which she mistakenly supposed sloshed within the bosom of Player B.

Player B referred to the Rules of Golf. 'I am sorry, dear,' she said with her serpent smile, 'but since a rattlesnake is not a man-made object, and therefore is not a movable obstruction, it must be either an outside agency or an impediment and you must not touch it in a hazard.'

The last thing Player A proposed to do was touch the rattlesnake but she was not comforted in the least by this ruling. 'I wondered,' she replied diffidently, 'if I might not get some relief. In a safe place. Well away from that creature.'

Player B feigned deepest shock at this suggestion. 'Relief? Your ball does not lie in casual water. It is not in ground under repair. By no stretch of the imagination could a rattlesnake be classified as freshly cut material piled for removal. Of course you could declare it unplayable and drop another ball in the hazard. But that will cost you a stroke and you wouldn't have a dog's chance of saving a half on the hole.'

'I do not want to drop another ball in the hazard. I do not want to go anywhere near the hazard,' said Player A.

'Oh, don't be such a ninny,' said Player B. 'I'll tell you what. You play the shot and I will stand by ready with the rake and whack the brute if it rears its ugly head. There must be a slight chance that I will get in a blow before it sinks its fatal venom into your leg.'

I have taken a certain licence in reconstructing this dialogue because my source material, the laconic account in the resulting USGA Decision, confines itself to a bare recital of the facts, but you get the idea. Incidentally, the committee decreed that the Rules of Golf do not require players to put themselves into physical danger and that in this instance Player A would have been justified in dropping a ball into another greenside bunker, *sans* rattlesnake, in a similar lie and at an equal distance from the flagstick.

Another snake, a cobra this time and wide awake, provided a complication for Jimmy Stewart on the third hole of the Bukit course during the 1972 Singapore Open. He drove off and as he walked up to the ball he noticed that this ten-foot cobra had the same idea, presumably thinking that the ball was an egg. With a deft blow Stewart dispatched the cobra and then, with the atonishment of a child playing with one of those Russian babushka dolls which reveal progressively smaller dolls inside each other, he saw to his horror another snake slither from the mouth of the cobra he had just killed. With what was now a practised swing he did for that one too.

That incident is recorded in the *Golfer's Handbook*, which is a positive mine of golfing curiosa.

I hope it gave them the bellyache

My own tenative flirtation with the glamorous world of big-time golf was prematurely curtailed by intervention from the animal world in the shape of a large red deer. It was during the Danish Open in Copenhagen and for some inexplicable reason one of my drives curled in flight and the ball missed the fairway, falling among a herd of deer grazing the lush rough. A big brute with spreading antlers consumed it at a gulp and my bid for international fame dissolved in the digestive juices of the importunate ruminant.

Uncharitable so-called friends have from time to time suggested that I invented that incident to excuse my failure to become a superstar. Deer, they suggest cruelly, do not eat golf balls. I refer them and other sceptics to the *Handbook* and the section headed 'Interference by Birds and Animals' which closely follows 'Spectators Interfering with Balls'. A herd of young bullocks, a cousin of the red deer please note, grazed on a pasture adjoining the Headingly golf club near Leeds and one of the animals had to be slaughtered because it was losing weight. Its stomach was found to contain 56 golf balls.

A gopher in Winnipeg had the same idea. Its nest was found to contain no fewer than 250 golf balls, neatly arranged in rows and packed in moss, stored up to provide sustenance during the winter on the supposition that they were eggs.

The documentation is rather sketchy but we can all relish the dismay of the golfer who chipped into the hole and whose delight was shattered when the ball popped out of the hole, followed by a bad-tempered frog which had been taking a siesta within the cup.

That was nothing compared with the experience of Mrs Molly Whitaker when she went to play out of a bunker on the Beachwood golf course in South Africa. A fully grown monkey leapt from nearby bushes and grabbed her round the neck. Your guess at its motives is as good as mine, and probably more suitable for a family audience. Her caddie beat it off with a club.

But for a really chilling incident, imagine yourself in the gallery of the final of the Welsh Girls' Championship at Abergale in 1978. Susan Rowlands is lining up her putt when a small mouse runs across the green and disappears up her trouser leg. Susan does not flicker an eyelid. She concentrates furiously and strokes the vital putt which was to take her on to eventual victory.

As she watches the ball drop into the hole the mouse runs down her trouser leg again and scampers off to safety. Goodness, what self-control and perfect absorption in the game. Compared with this performance, the famous incident of Joyce Wethered holing out with an express thundering by and afterwards asking 'What train?' pales into insignificance. When Susan Rowlands was congratulated on her steely nerve she said that she had not been aware of the mouse's hickory dickory dock performance. That is real concentration. 'What mouse?'

Prudence is the best policy

How can you tell whether a rattlesnake is dead or asleep or, possibly even wide awake and fractious and just pretending to be asleep?

These questions presented themselves to Wade Cagle for urgent consideration in the gloaming of a spring evening when he almost stepped on the coiled mass of a large rattler near a green on the eve of the New Orleans Open.

As PGA Tournament supervisor it was Cagle's task to inspect the course and determine which were the water hazards, as opposed to lateral water hazards, define the course boundaries, and decide whether there were any parts of the course unsuitable for the proper playing of golf.

The shock of seeing the snake caused him to challenge the world record for a standing, backwards long-jump and he stood for some while at a safe distance turning over those questions in his mind. He toyed briefly with the idea of throwing pebbles at the serpent, but rejected the plan on the grounds of prudence.

One of the chief requirements for the job of tournament supervisor is a thorough knowledge of the Rules of Golf and Cagle recalled a Decision in which the judgement stated without equivocation that the rules never required a player to put himself into physical danger. That dictum carried the force of an article of basic human rights, overriding all rules in the same way that a citizen is absolved from observing the laws forbidding assault and battery in defending himself from a murderous attack.

Cagle reasoned that it was his clear duty to protect the golfers. By extension, that Decision could probably be stretched to cover tournament supervisors. It was probably only by oversight that the Rules of Golf Committee had omitted to mention tournament supervisors in its ruling.

With infinite caution he approached the snake with a can of aerosol paint held up in front of him, in the manner of vampire-hunter extending a crucifix. Keeping a safe distance from the creature, he gingerly walked backwards around the snake, spraying a white line on the turf. The encircled snake was now officially designated as ground under repair, a no-go zone affording free relief for the players. Cagle quickly sought the safety of his electric cart and sped to the clubhouse.

There was a postscript to this deed of imagination and daring above and beyond the call of duty. In the morning the green-keeper assigned to mow the green saw a white circle around the snake he had killed the previous day. Casually he picked up the carcase and tossed it into the bushes.

Bum's rush for a bush pig

In layman's terms the African bush pig is a scaled down version of the wart hog. It carries its tail stuck straight up into the air, like an aerial, and I lay some stress on this fact to provide a clue to what follows since a natural delicacy precludes me from being too specific. The bush pig, I should add, is wild – and never wilder than during a painful episode on the Elephant Hills golf course at Victoria Falls in what is now Zimbabwe.

Nicky Price, who was to come so close to winning the 1982 Open Championship at Royal Troon, had just completed his national service with the Rhodesian army and was anxious to get his swing back into working order. It was at Elephant Hills that he exchanged his rifle for the more familiar weapons of golf, his first round for many months. His game proved to be under-standably rusty but he felt he was getting the hang of it again and he saw no reason to delay his tee shot when a family of bush pigs trotted diagonally across the fairway ahead of him, led by the proud father.

Price caught the ball thin and, although it departed like a bullet, it never rose above 18 inches from the ground. The ball caught the large male bush pig precisely at the base of the aerial and disappeared, or plugged as golfers say. The bush pig emitted a shriek of pain and anger and took off at high speed for the bush, with its tribe in squealing pursuit.

The terror of the bush pigs was matched only by the horror of the golfers playing adjacent fairways as the stampede of screaming beasts made their unswerving rush from the outrage of man's playground.

6

The law according to Murphy

Fate keeps on happening

Anita Loos

Excusez-moi, je suis Anglais

French is bad enough, using the same word for 'above' and 'below'. Oh, I know that one is *au dessus* and the other *en dessous* but since in their slipshod Gallic way the French abbreviate both to a sound resembling a sudden puncturing of a waterbed, a sort of 'dssew', it is impossible for the English ear to detect any distinction in meaning. Most of the time I am indifferent to what the French say, or how they say it, although I suspect that they themselves have problems with this semantic ambiguity from time to time, not excluding the occasional puncturing of a waterbed. All would be well if they would speak slowly and clearly, the way I am always telling them to, especially at golf tournaments. Communication in the golf fraternity is invariably related to par, including the quality of the steaks in the clubhouse and assessments of the charms of the waitresses, and I still blush to recall an incident at a French Open Championship. I was walking the course, en route to pick up the leader, and on the way I met Jean Garaialde who had just completed nine holes.

'What is it that passes itself, my brave?' I inquired politely. (It sounds fractionally better in French.)

'Sept dssew,' he replied gravely.

'Holy blue!' I exclaimed enthusiastically. 'It is formidable, that. Go France!'

Imagine my chagrin some time later when I inspected the scoreboard and saw that Garaialde, far from being seven under par, was seven over.

In revenge for that embarrassment I just hope that this book goes into French translation and that they get into an equal tangle over the difference between the phrase 'One of those days' and the expression which means the exact opposite: 'One of *those* days'.

This chapter has absolutely nothing to do with one of those days, the rare occasions when every putt drops and you begin to suspect that you might have been mistaken in believing that your driver is possessed of a bloody-minded will of its own. No, this chapter is devoted to one of *those* days, such as the occasion when Steve Melnyk flew 4000 miles to Hawaii only to discover that he had forgotten to enter for the Hawaiian Open. Or when Lance Percival put his tee shot six inches from the cup in the Dunlop Masters pro-am, being in receipt of a handicap stroke on the hole, and was robbed of his moment of team glory within seconds as the pro, Manual Pinero, holed out with his tee shot. Or when Glen Mason and Ronnie Carroll booked a golf holiday in Mallorca and on arrival took a taxi directly to the course. The driver delivered them to a mini-golf course in the centre of Palma, since the real golf course described in the holiday brochure had not been built. The two singers duly played mini-golf, using their full sets of clubs, including the drivers, to propel their balls through windmills and into the mouths of clowns.

There, *mes amis*, you have examples of one of *those* days although they all pale to insignificance compared with the experience of two club golfers in Northern Ireland.

Well, there's just one more thing

In the late seventies Hammy Gillespie had to make an embarrassing call on the wife of his golfing companion, Jimmy Donnelly. The conversation went something like this:

Mrs Donnelly: 'Hello, Hammy. I thought you were out playing golf with Jimmy at Royal Belfast.'

Hammy: 'No, it was Holywood. Yes, we were playing golf. That is what I called about.'

Mrs Donnelly: 'Is something wrong?'

Hammy: 'Well, Jimmy had a bit of a mishap.'

Mrs Donnelly: 'What happened? Is he all right?'

Hammy: 'It was a pure accident. You see, Jimmy was bending down to tie his shoelace on the tee only I did not know he was bending down to tie his shoelace. He was behind me. Well, I took a practice swing just as Jimmy bent down. . . .'

Mrs Donnelly: 'And?'

Hammy: 'My club caught him a glancing blow on the head.'

Mrs Donnelly: 'Oh my God. Is his head badly injured?'

Hammy: 'No, no. It was not much more than a tap, really. Just made him groggy for a minute or two.'

Mrs Donnelly: 'Then why isn't he here with you?'

Hammy: 'Obviously I was concerned for Jimmy and I thought it would be best to have someone take a look at him. After all, you never know with bangs on the head. Better be safe than sorry. So I picked him up in a fireman's lift to take him back to the clubhouse.'

Mrs Donnelly: 'And the doctor found a fractured skull?'

Hammy: 'No, I told you. His head is fine. Just a bump and maybe a touch of concussion. Nothing to worry about.'

Mrs Donnelly: 'So?'

Hammy: 'Unfortunately, while I was carrying him to the clubhouse I tripped and Jimmy's ankle got hurt.'

Mrs Donnelly: 'What kind of hurt?'

Hammy: 'Compound fracture, actually, although I didn't know that at the time. Well, I got him to the clubhouse without further problems and we called the ambulance. They took him to hospital.'

Mrs Donnelly: 'Is that all?'

Hammy: 'Not quite. You know how Jimmy feels about his car. Thinks the world of that new Audi, like a kid with a new toy. Well, I thought that after all that had happened it would be the least I could do to drive his car to the hospital and then bring it here. So you could keep an eye on it. It would be safe here, better than stuck in the car park at the club.'

Mrs Donnelly: 'Never mind about the car, I am worried about Jimmy. You've smashed his head in and broken his ankle. Is that the limit of the injuries you have done to him?'

Hammy: 'By the sheerest mischance there was another slight contretemps on the way to the hospital.'

Mrs Donnelly: 'Sweet Mother of Mary, tell me. What else?'

Hammy: 'You know how the traffic is in Belfast. The ambulance driver had to slam on the brakes and I did not have a chance. Believe me, nobody could have stopped and the car sort of bumped into the back of the ambulance.'

Mrs Donnelly: 'Tell me what you mean by sort of bumped into the back of the ambulance?'

Hammy: 'Well, the impact must have damaged the catch and the doors flew open. . . .'

Mrs Donnelly: 'And?'

Hammy: 'The stretcher slid off its runners and Jimmy fell into the road.'

Mrs Donnelly: 'He's dead! You've killed him!'

Hammy: 'Not at all. He just broke his collar bone. Collar bones are nothing, Mrs Donnelly, rugby players break them all the time. Jimmy will be up and about again in a matter of months.'

Mrs Donnelly: 'Is there no end to it? Tell me frankly if that is everything – broken head, shock, concussion, fractured ankle and smashed collar bone.'

Hammy: 'Believe me, Mrs Donnelly, that is absolutely the full extent of the damage so far as Jimmy is concerned.'

Mrs Donnelly: 'So far as Jimmy is concerned? Were there other victims of your murderous rampage?'

Hammy: 'Not people, no. But there was the car. . . .'

Mrs Donnelly: 'Ah, yes, the sort of bump with the ambulance. Is the fender bent?'

Hammy: 'Well, yes it is, as it happens. But. . . .'

Mrs Donnelly: 'But what?'

Hammy: 'I am afraid that it is a complete write-off.'

Sequel: Hammy Gillespie and Jimmy Donnelly are still good friends and continue to play golf regularly at Holywood.

Some days you just can't win

Allan Robertson was the first golf pro and his sterling qualities provided an example which set the highest standards for the new profession. There is no absolute proof that Robertson was the first man to state that 'the mark of a professional golfer is the ability to contain his score while playing badly' but the presumption is strong. After all, the observation is so blindingly obvious that it is most unlikely that the first professional would fail to utter words to that effect at some time. Robertson was one of those strong, silent Scots who have the ability to keep a straight face while uttering a crushing banality and this talent tends to invest their fatuities with the aura of deepest insight, nay wisdom. Students of this phenomenon who wish to pursue their studies are recommended to the literary works of Sir Walter Scott. And good luck to them.

Even if Robertson was not the original culprit there is no doubting that the postulation about holding a score together while playing badly was one of the earliest articles of faith of professional golf and was handed down from generation to generation, in due course crossing the Atlantic to the New World. There the adage spawned a host of colloquial clichés, like 'You drive for show and putt for dough' and 'Getting up and down from the ball washer'.

The Palmers are a conservative family and I like to think that it was Deacon Palmer who passed down the expression in its pure, original form to the youthful Arnold Palmer, possibly with the added emphasis of a clip round the ear. At any rate, the Sage of Latrobe gave public expression to this sacred tenet of golf philosophy and thereby inspired new generations of young professionals.

It is all very well to exhort golfers to stick to their task and keep grafting away when their swings are out of kilter but how can you give aid and comfort to the player whose swing is in perfect working order? After all, it would be ludicrous to put a fatherly hand on a young player's shoulder, look him straight in the eye and say: 'Son, the mark of a professional golfer is the ability to contain his score while playing *well*.' The occasions when a pro golfer needs a resounding cliché to sustain his morale while striking the ball superbly are not as rare as you might imagine. Hark to the chastening tale of none other than Jack Nicklaus in the Bing Crosby National Pro-am at Pebble Beach in 1976.

Nicklaus was right on top of his game. His thinking was sharp, his tactical sense acute. He was, therefore, leading the tournament after 63 holes and inexorably headed for his fourth Crosby title. Or so it seemed, especially on Nicklaus's favourite course.

Responsible critics were mystified by what happened next. One wrote of Nicklaus playing an inexcusably bad iron shot, another suggested that a recent skiing holiday had affected his golfing muscles, a third that a new set of irons was to blame. Nothing of the sort, insists Nicklaus himself. He concentrated hard on every shot and executed them all to the limit of his ability. The problem was that on those nine holes he was visited by a freakish sequence of what golfers loosely term rubs of the green. Luck in golf is supposed to even itself out, and possibly it does over the span of a year or so, but on this occasion fate threw the lot at him.

The chapter of horrors began at the 13th where a huge drive finished in a fairway lie which was more of a pothole than a divot scrape. The 'inexcusably bad shot' was actually about the best shot that Nicklaus or anyone else could have fashioned. The ball finished on a bare area under the lee of a buried stone. His chip from this dire spot was a marvel of precision. The ball failed by inches to crest the mound guarding the green and rolled back. Instead of a tap-in for par Nicklaus had a guiltless six.

And so it went on. At the par-three 17th his tee shot was perfect when it left the clubface. A capricious gust of wind knocked the ball into the front bunker. After his series of bizarre bounces, horrendous lies and putts deflected by heel marks, Nicklaus was prepared for the worst. Sure enough his ball was deeply buried in the sand. He made a good swing and the ball scuttled 12 inches, into a crevice. Double-bogey five.

At the last hole he had to go for the green with a massive second shot. With the fates in their malicious mood the lie of the ball on the fairway was, to say the least, dubious. With all his experience Nicklaus could not predict how the ball would fly from such an unpromising launching pad. He made good contact and looked up. Sure enough the ball was swinging towards the beach. By this time Nicklaus had long since exhausted any feelings of frustration or anger. The plot had developed from tragedy to a rollicking black farce and he responded appropriately with laughter. If the laugh was at his own expense it was no less genuine for all that. He played out the hole brilliantly, as anyone must from the beach on this hole to salvage a seven. That put him home in 45, level bogeys, for a share of 18th place and $2200 instead of the $37,000 which two hours earlier had seemed to be safely in the bank. Who was it who said that golf is a humbling game? Come to think of it, it was probably Allan Robertson.

A question of vegetation

Mark Lye was given a set of golf clubs at the age of nine and lived happily ever after. As a biography that may be rather sketchy but it covers the essentials. No fairy godmother's gift was ever more valuable than those clubs. They marked his destiny, resolved all dilemmas about the future and endowed him with health, wealth and happiness. There were setbacks along the way, as there always must be with the game of golf, but Mark had the world by the tail on a downhill pull and he knew it.

The tall Californian turned professional in 1975 and was in no way perturbed by his initial failure to win his player's card. This was not failure so much as an opportunity to see the world while pursuing his chosen career. In those days Europe was the place because, strange as it may seem today, the word 'Open' meant just that, in the sense that the Open tournaments were open to any *bona fide* professional with a set of clubs and the price of the entry fee. Young Lye tried without success to qualify for the Swiss and Scandinavian Opens, and then he returned home to be honoured at the banquet for collegiate All-Americans, on the strength of his amateur successes for San José State University.

It was two o'clock on the morning of the first round of the German Open when Lye arrived back in Europe at Bremen, not the most auspicious preparation for golf. Over the early holes of Dr von Limburger's masterpiece the lassitude of jet-lag made Lye swing at a languorous three-quarters power and his golf prospered. After 15 holes he was leading the tournament.

He then encountered heather, an experience which is invariably unnerving on first acquaintance. Heather looks innocuous enough; there is no visible sign in those innocent purple flowers and luxuriant fronds that the plant is constructed of a material akin to tempered steel.

Lye attempted a normal pitch shot, as if playing from grass. To his astonishment the ball moved about a yard, and nestled deeper into the heather. Half a dozen wrist-jarring shots later he got his ball out and completed the hole for a nine.

On the next hole he drove into the noble trees which are the chief hazard of Bremen golf club and by this time Lye's capacity for rational thought was thoroughly diminished. The woods echoed with the staccato sound of high-compression golf ball meeting high-compression beech-tree, and then with the falsetto squeal of his caddie reacting to a direct hit on the shin bone from a ricochet. Lye's baptism of professional golf was completed by a second successive nine.

Strange to relate, he made the cut.

If ever there was a sure-fire bet. . . .

Without going too deeply into the philosophical implications of ill winds which blow nobody any good, it is obvious that one man's disaster may well be another man's triumph. As an example we could do no better than go back to a fine June evening in 1926 and join the members in the companionable bar of the Glamorganshire golf club.

They were enjoying well-deserved pints of beer after toiling round the comely links of Penarth when in walked the dapper figure of the national golfing hero, Henry Howell. His ears may well have been burning because Henry was frequently the subject of conversation in the bar, either because of his exploits on the course as captain of the Welsh team or because of his nocturnal escapades, for Henry was a bit of a lad, a real card. There were lots of stories about Henry well worth discussion, many of them prompting admiring chuckles among the men. When these tales were recounted later in the privacy of their bedchambers the womenfolk tended to purse their lips in shock while their eyes glazed over and took on that far-away look of secret dreams.

On this occasion we may conjecture that the conversation was about whether Henry intended to win the Howell Cup, a trophy presented to the club by his father for a tournament which required competitors to qualify for the final stages by putting in three cards. The issue was straightforward. Henry had submitted two good cards and if he chose to play a third qualifying round it was a foregone conclusion that he would go on and win the cup. But this was the last day for qualifying and there was not much daylight left.

How about it, Henry? Well, he said, he might go out if he could find a caddie. There was no shortage of volunteers to carry the clubs of the plus-3 demigod. Could he get round before dark? Oh, easily, said Henry. An hour and a half should be ample.

You might rush round in 90 minutes, granted, said a self-confessed expert on golfing matters, but you couldn't hope to do much of a score at that pace. Henry's well-developed Sky Masterson instincts stirred at these challenging words. 'Oh, I don't know about that; I think I could probably do 70 in 90 minutes.' 'I'll give you 5 to 1 against a 70 in 90 minutes,' said the sage. 'And I will have a pound at those odds,' replied Henry. It should be remembered that in 1926 a pound represented a whole day's pay for a skilled craftsman.

Since Henry was comfortably off as the son of a prosperous draper it seemed to the members that Christmas had come early that year. Here was the chance of a lifetime to participate in the socialist panacea of redistribution of wealth. What about 6 to 1 against breaking 70 in 90 minutes asked a member who had long and painful experience of the Penarth bunkers. 'You're on,' said Henry.

Now everyone wanted to get into the act, offering ever more extravagant odds for ever more extravagant proposals. A friend offered to cover Henry's losses so he calmly accepted all the wagers, right down to the proposal of one comedian who suggested 40 to 1 against a score of 65 in 70 minutes.

The total of all those quids, ten bobs and half crowns was by now considerable and the thing had to be done properly. They chose one of their number to act as official marker, on the grounds of his undoubted probity and the fact that he was completely sober. The same criteria was applied to the selection of a timekeeper. Off they went to the first tee and the members ordered another round of drinks in anticipation of their windfalls.

On that June evening in the year of Our Lord 1926 Henry Rupert Howell went round the 6000 yard Glamorganshire golf course in 63 strokes and precisely 68 minutes.

Almost beyond human endurance

The philosophy behind the design of the Augusta National golf club's course, as devised by Bobby Jones and his co-architect, Dr Alister Mackenzie, was that it should be an enjoyable course for every level of golfer and a difficult challenge for the expert seeking to make birdies. The result is a course with generously wide fairways, almost double the width of other championship courses, and large greens. It is, then, not difficult for a competent player to keep his ball in play and hit the greens in the regulation number of strokes. Then the fun begins. The greens slope or undulate extravagantly so the player looking for a birdie must hit an approach shot of exquisite precision, stopping his ball to leave a short and uphill putt. Therein lies the essence of Augusta, and in order to preserve this paramount characteristic the surfaces must be fast, very fast.

The climate of Georgia, with its extremes of temperature during the changing seasons, is hostile to grass, and it takes all the skills of the greens staff to produce immaculate putting surfaces for the Masters every April. Indeed, during the seventies two varieties of resilient grasses were used on the greens to guarantee a good growth in the springtime. Well, the grass was green enough and the putting surfaces were true enough but they were, by Augusta standards, slow, too slow to preserve the integrity of the original design concept. It was therefore ordained that for the 1982 Masters the greens should be reseeded with the bent grass which would provide slick putting surfaces, even though Augusta was beyond the natural growing limits of this strain.

This quest for fast greens succeeded beyond all expectations. Indeed the 1982 Masters was marked by unseemly giggles from the hapless players at the antics played by putts on those glassy surfaces. Jack Nicklaus had a two-foot putt on the 16th and he knew with absolute certainty that if he missed the cup the ball would roll on and on down the slope and into the pond. Competitors were lagging putts of 10 and 12 feet just to be sure of getting home with the next one. There were places on some of the more severe slopes where a putt as delicate as the stroke of a butterfly's wing on the ball would start it off on a 40-foot trundle down the green.

The 18th green was a case in point. Ask Mark Hayes. He hit a splendid, attacking shot to the flag and his ball finished no more than seven feet from the hole. His putt was across and slightly down the slope and the ball wavered as it touched the edge of the rim and then rolled past. It almost stopped six feet below the hole but after a momentary hesitation it took another turn, picked up momentum and rolled on and on right off the front of the green.

Hayes was dumbfounded, and angry at the involuntary sniggers from the gallery. He now had a 35-foot putt back to the green and played a beauty, judged to perfection. The ball rolled up to the hole, made a U-turn behind it and then retraced its route all the way back to Hayes's feet. This was altogether too ludicrous for the spectators to maintain their traditional respectful silence at a player's misfortunes. 'It was kind of hard to take when you are trying as hard as you can and people are laughing at you,' said Hayes afterwards.

He tried again, lagging the putt up to five feet short of the hole and chasing after the ball so that he would be able to hit it again the moment it stopped, before it decided to yield to its inertia and roll back again. They gave him a sympathetic cheer when he holed the next one for a six, but he was not amused. After all, instead of the birdie which would have put him right into contention he was back in the pack.

Mullins' big splash

Moon Mullins never reached the lucrative heights of the American Tour but during his time among the arid foothills of golf he earned himself a permanent place in the locker-room lore of professional golf. He was playing the Jacksonville Open and by mischance hit his ball into a man-made water hazard with a sloping concrete bank.

By standing in the water he could contrive a shot at the partially submerged ball, and in due course did so, to the accompaniment of a mighty splash. Like a good pro, Mullins played an attacking stroke, accelerating the clubhead through the ball and completing the swing with a high follow-through. At this point in the proceedings it seemed to the onlookers that Mullins had suffered an attack of total paralysis, or just possibly, that he had been turned into a pillar of salt.

At all events, he stood there holding the pose of a classic high finish. Not a muscle moved. Then, ever so slowly, Mullins began to disappear. Like a ship being launched down a slipway, Mullins slid backwards down the concrete slope, still holding that high finish with the rigidity of a statue. The only sign of animation he displayed was a slight popping of his eyes as the spikes of his shoes lost their purchase on the slimy concrete and he slid gently into the deep. When he was eventually retrieved from the hazard he explained that he had been afraid of losing his balance if he moved.

Half of golf is fun, the other half is putting

The origins of golf have not been established with certainty and probably never will be. However, if we ponder the appeal of the game, the variety and magnificence of the natural settings in which golf is played, man's communion with nature, the healthy benefits he derives from striding purposefully over verdant fairways and inhaling unpolluted air, the exhilaration amounting to a spiritual experience he enjoys from the sharp retort of brassie meeting ball, the harmony of body and soul in the vision of a nine-iron shot arcing against an azure sky straight at the flag, and the intoxication of feeling that it is wonderful to be alive as a doughty opponent extends his hand in congratulations at a worthy victory, then it is difficult to contest the theory that half of golf at least was God's gift to humanity. In that case the other half of golf, the putting, must have been the Devil's contribution.

The act of rolling a ball into a hole 4¼ inches in diameter has wrought such havoc among golfers that it has on occasion prompted murderous assaults, suicides, divorces and confinement in institutions. There is nothing in the whole world of sport which produces such extremes of emotion in the players as the black art of putting. Bobby Locke, who achieved a relationship with his putter akin to the rapport between lovers, took the club to bed with him. Ky Laffoon, on the other hand, trailed his putter on a string behind his car to punish it for its manifest wickedness. Mark James, the English Ryder Cup player, became convinced that his putter was possessed of an evil spirit and in an amateurish attempt at exorcism kicked it round a car park and then threw it into a bush to spend the night in contemplation of its sins. Walter Hagen seriously considered asking the Pope to bless his putter.

It is depressing to review the horror stories of putting, which are legion, and it may also be dangerous to probe too deeply into the world of the occult. When Max Faulkner won the Open

Championship of 1951 he brazenly announced that he would never miss a three-foot putt again as long as he lived. The writer Henry Longhurst moved away lest the gods took him for an accomplice in this blasphemy.

For contemporary golfers the most painful putting incident was probably the missed three-footer which cost Doug Sanders the Open of 1970 on the last green at St Andrews. That memory is still recent and the hurt lingers, but it was by no means the most blatant error to blow a championship.

Harry Vardon missed a six-inch putt in the US Open of 1913 and as a result of his carelessness he finished in a three-way tie and lost in the play-off to Francis Ouimet. Any advance on six inches? Certainly. Let us go back to 1889 and the Open Championship at Musselburgh. In the last round Andrew Kirkaldy and Willie Park were disputing the title and on the 14th green Kirkaldy made a one-handed pass with his putter at the ball which lay *one inch* from the hole. He missed the ball entirely and it was by the margin of that one stroke that he finished in a tie, subsequently to lose the play-off.

Probably the most profligate putting performance by an experienced tournament professional occurred during the 1968 French Open Championship at St Cloud. Brian Barnes, reputed to have one of the surest putting strokes in British golf, made a mess of his play of the short eighth hole during the second round and he was lying three when he faced a putt of one yard. He was, in the current jargon, hot, and became considerably hotter when this bogey putt failed to find its target.

A crimson penumbra obscured his view of the hole as he stuck out his putter to rake the ball into the cup and, like a playful puppy entering into the spirit of a game, the ball once more escaped its fate. At this point the action began to quicken, almost to a blur in the evidence of the transfixed eye-witnesses. Barnes, who had been an accomplished hockey-player in his youth, patted the ball violently to and fro, hopping about the while to avoid striking himself on the foot. He even contrived to play one stroke while standing astride the line of his putt, thereby adding the insult of two penalty strokes under Rule 35-1L to the injury of his self-esteem.

His astonished marker, frantically trying to keep score with this dervishlike performance, made it 11 putts from three feet.

Barnes demurred violently. 'Well,' said the marker, 'when you catch your ass in a buzz-saw it is not too easy to tell how many teeth bit you. What did you make it?'

'Twelve!' snapped Barnes, departing at high speed in the direction of the Aeroport de Charles de Gaulle.

As for the Sanders tragedy, this splendid man has a resilient spirit which has survived the trauma of missing out on his chance of winning a major championship. At the time it was, of course, a crippling kick in the guts but he looks back without dismay or reproach and remembers mostly the warmth of the public sympathy and encouragement he received. He can even appreciate the stories he has heard of his caddie selling the actual ball which missed the putt which lost the Open, not just once but with true entrepreneurial flair 20 times over.

Not so much a rub, more a thump of the green

Bobby Cruickshank was a small, wiry Scot and his promising amateur career was interrupted by the First World War. He escaped from a German prisoner-of-war camp and soon after the war he turned professional and emigrated to the United States where he quickly won a reputation as a fine player and all-round athlete.

In the 1934 US Open Championship at Merion, Philadelphia, he was leading after two rounds and going well in the third round. His approach to the 11th hole was slightly spared and to his dismay he saw the ball falling short into the brook which winds in front of the green.

The ball landed on a rock which was barely covered by water, rebounded high into the air and landed on the green. Cruickshank jubilantly tossed his club into the air, tipped his cap and shouted 'Thank you, God.' Further expressions of gratitude were cut short as the descending club landed on top of his head and knocked him out cold. He recovered his senses but not the impetus of his play and finished third.

To be absolutely precise he finished joint third, along with Whiffy Cox who also lost his very promising chance to win the championship because of a cruel quirk of fate. Fate in this instance took the form of a spectator who was sitting in his shirt-sleeves by the 12th green, enjoying the sunshine and the passing

parade of great golfers. His coat was spread on the ground beside him and Cox's ball landed on it. The man jumped to his feet, snatching his coat in an involuntary reflex action. The ball rolled out of bounds. The rules official decreed that Cox must follow the stroke and distance procedure. These days a stationary ball moved by an outside agency must be replaced and such an incident would create no problem, but in Cox's case the ruling was the equivalent of a two-stroke penalty. It was by two strokes that he failed to tie Olin Dutra and thus earn a chance of victory. Disasters are not confined to high scores, not by any means. It is possible for a golfer to have everything go right, to drive like a field gun, to pepper the flag with his approaches and sink more than his fair share of birdie putts and still end the day with a damp towel wrapped round his head and anguished groans issuing from his tormented soul.

Don't worry about this Blancas

So far as golf was concerned Fred Marti was the big man on the campus of the University of Houston and he was greatly encouraged by his golf-enthusiast father, who insisted that Fred call home each evening during a competition and report progress.

Marti followed this regular procedure when he entered the Premier Invitational at Longview, Texas, a reasonably demanding course with a par of 70. The conversation went something like this:

'Hi, dad.'

'Freddy, boy! How did it go?'

'Pretty good, dad. I made a few birdies.'

'Don't kid around, son. What did you shoot?'

'It was a 61, dad.'

'Jumping Jehosophat! A 61 eh? How many shots does that put you in the lead, Fred?'

'Actually I'm one shot back, dad.'

'You're kidding.'

'No, dad. Another of the guys from U of H shot 60.'

'Who the heck was that?'

'He's called Homero Blancas. His dad's a greenkeeper at the

River Oaks Country Club here in Houston and he's hardly had a club out of his hands since he was five years old.'

'Listen, Fred, one hot round means nothing. It could happen to anybody. The name of the game is consistency. Just you go out and put together another nice score and don't worry about this Blancas. I bet that was just a flash in the pan.'

'OK, dad. I'll call you tomorrow.'

'Right. And good luck, son.'

The following evening Fred Marti duly telephoned his father again, with the ensuing dialogue:

'Hi, dad.'

'Give it to me straight, Freddy. What did you do?'

'I shot another 61 for 122, dad.'

'Read 'em and weep! Can you imagine that, 61, 61. Son, I am proud of you. You're going to make a great professional. I know I told you to keep it consistent but I never dreamt of another 61. Congratulations, son. I'm just sorry I couldn't be there to see you receive the trophy. I bet that Blancas was sick when you threw another 61 at him.'

'Not so that you would notice, dad.'

'He finished close, huh?'

'No, dad, we were separated by seven strokes.'

'What did I tell you – right out of the money.'

'No, dad, he won.'

'How could he win if you shot 61? Were you disqualified or something?'

'No, my 61 was good.'

'Well then?'

'You see, dad, he just went out and shot a 55.'

The luck of the Irish

It would be quite possible to write an entire book about the disasters of Irish golf, although impractical with printing costs being the way they are, because in Ireland quite simple tasks, such as posting a letter, can involve adventures of a sublime and/or horrendous nature.

A fairly typical example of the Irish factor is evident in the story of Mike Souchak when he flew from America to play Bobby Cole in the film series 'Shell's Wonderful World of Golf'.

Souchak was able to undertake this engagement only on condition that the organizers would get him onto a plane back to New York that same night, because he had a very important engagement which demanded his prompt return.

Everything was meticulously arranged and as Souchak completed his round a car was waiting outside the Killarney clubhouse, the engine running, and the experienced driver briefed to go like the very wind to Shannon Airport. All went well. Souchak jumped into the car and the car departed in a cloud of dust and soon the driver was reassuring Souchak that sure they could get there and back in half the time. Souchak relaxed. Indeed, remarked the driver, they had so much time in hand that it would be possible for them to halt briefly to pay respects to his cousin, a man renowned throughout the emerald isle for the quality of his poteen. In fact, it would be a criminal waste of the chance of a lifetime not to halt briefly. Souchak concurred and three days later it took three strong men to push him up the steps of a homebound plane.

Since Ireland measures only about 300 miles by 150 miles, the inhabitants tend to complacency in the matter of travel. The longest journey is just down the road and this offhand notion of distance was behind the plan of Roddy Carr, Des Smyth and Warren Humphreys to drive to the south of Portugal for the Portuguese Open Championship.

Furthermore, since there were three drivers and they had all read *Marathon Man* in the recent past, they would do the drive non-stop. They met in London, drove to Dover and crossed by ferry to Boulogne. The marathon men were on their way, armed with a rudimentary map of Europe about the size of a postcard on which their journey represented a run of about five inches.

For the first 14 hours or so they made fair progress, by dint of keeping the sun shining in the left-hand windows during the morning and the right-hand windows in the afternoon. As the sun began to set they saw the mighty Pyrenees rising ahead and shortly they were halted by a traffic jam. They stopped a truck with British licence plates which was coming the other way and the driver told them that an avalanche had closed the road ahead. It would not be clear for 24 hours or so in his opinion.

The three golfers decided to proceed as they would back home, go back a bit and find a road which would make a detour around the obstruction. They found a road which seemed to go in the right direction and soon they were climbing steeply up the mountains. As they drove into the night the traffic became thinner and the snow thicker. The road also grew markedly narrower, as did the gap between the needle on their fuel gauge and the 'empty' mark. As they reached each crest they prayed that the road, by now no more than a track, would descend into a hospitable plain, amply furnished with restaurants and filling stations, but the mountains loomed ever more menacingly. All three of them recalled reading about car passengers becoming stranded and freezing to death in their vehicles. By now the only sign of civilization of any kind was the wheel tracks of a single vehicle in the snow. They saw it ahead of them, stopped by the roadside. It was a lorry fitted with a snowplough.

The golfers threw themselves on the driver's mercy. He proved to be a man with a merciful soul and towed them over passes which would have been quite beyond the capacity of their car to negotiate, even if it had not run out of fuel.

Finally they descended into Spain and were able to refill the tank. They were chilled to the marrow of their bones but nothing would deflect them from their purpose of making the trip without stopping. On they went through the night and into the morning and on to Madrid. Carr wanted to stop and rest, claiming that his view had precedence over democratic decisions on the grounds that it was his car. The others scoffed at this effete suggestion. How could they hope to succeed as professional golfers if they allowed themselves to be deflected from their purpose? The only concession they permitted was a slight revision in the original plan, which was to call in at Sotogrande on the way to say hello to Carr's father, the great Joe Carr, who was there on holiday. It had seemed to involve a detour of an inch or so on their map but when they discovered that it would add about 500 miles to the trip they pressed on to Portugal.

They made it but their triumph was marred by the fact that all three had high fevers. Smyth and Humphreys had to withdraw and return home by more conventional long-distance transport. Carr had to live with his influenza because somebody had to take the car back. The original scheme to drive all round Europe's tournament circuit was ruined – and never revived by these three players.

They say it broadens the mind

Others were not deterred by the example of the Irish fiasco, notably Brian Sharrock. He missed the halfway cut in the Madrid Open Championship and so the next order of business was to get himself off to the site of the next tournament. That's one thing about missing a cut; it gives you a chance to get to know the next course and to work on your game. In theory, that is. The next tournament in this instance was the Italian Open Championship, to be played at Is Molas on the southern coast of Sardinia.

Sharrock had heard that there was a ferry from Marseilles to Sardinia and he calculated that if he hustled he could just make it. He threw his clubs into the car and drove through the night to Barcelona, a distance of some 800 miles. Here he paused briefly, sleeping for four hours on the floor of a friend's apartment, and then he was off on the road again, covering the 700 miles to Marseilles in good time for the ferry's scheduled departure. Ferry to Sardinia? Of course there is a ferry. It sails every Tuesday morning. So much for the locker-room grapevine on the subject of European travel. What about air travel? There were no flights to Sardinia from Marseilles but there was a flight to the island of Corsica the next morning. Corsica assuredly was a step in the right direction. But would there be any way of getting from Corsica to Sardinia? *Certainement, monsieur*, there are ferries. Sharrock deposited his car in the long-term parking lot, bought a ticket to Corsica and found himself a cheap room for the night.

The Sunday morning flight to Corsica was without incident and, while he would now have less time to prepare himself for the Italian Open, he had no cause for concern about making his Monday morning starting time for the prequalifying round. Corsica was under heavy rain and high winds as Sharrock bounced along in a country bus, bound for the southern port of Santa Margarita whence the Sardinian ferries were alleged to sail. So they did in fine weather, although not on the Sabbath. Now Sharrock began to worry. He was on the wrong island in the middle of the Mediterranean, standing forlornly on the seafront in lashing rain and gathering darkness and he was due on the tee in 12 hours. The situation called for a raid on his dwindling reserves of cash to restore his flagging spirits. He walked into a bar frequented by the fishermen and ordered a morale-booster. The barman was a fully paid-up member of the international order of unofficial analysts and psychotherapists and recognized a soul in torment. He inquired if the young man had a problem. Sharrock explained his predicament and asked if there was perhaps a fisherman who might, for a consideration, take him to Sardinia. The barman called across to a grizzled veteran and negotiations began. The man operated a small pleasure craft which normally plied along the coast with day-trippers seated uncomfortably on wooden slatted seats, taking photographs and drinking rough red wine.

The bargaining was protracted. The boatman played his hand with the skill of a true bandito. It is not for nothing that the Mafia started, and still flourishes, in Corsica. He was tired. The day had been hard and long. The seas were dangerously high and the journey perilous. Sharrock had no choice but to accede to the man's extortionate demands. His one stipulation was that they must sail immediately and that the destination must be the south of Sardinia. Finally, they spat on their palms and shook hands on the deal. The tiny craft bobbed on the heaving waves as they chugged into the night.

The journey was uncomfortable but without incident. As the boatman made fast to a jetty in the inky blackness he indicated that there was a bus stop just along the road, took his money and disappeared quickly into the night. At that moment Sharrock realized that he was on the northernmost coast of Sardinia. The good luck which had been conspicuously absent from his travels so far now came to his aid in rich measure. He hitch-hiked to the bus stop, arriving just in time to catch a bus, which deposited him at a railway station within minutes of the departure of a milk train. The sun was up by the time the train pulled into Cagliari after the four-hour train journey, but the promise of a generous tip brought out the latent racing talents in the taxi driver, and the last four miles to Is Molas were covered in record time, leaving Sharrock several minutes to lace up his spikes before striking his first drive. He missed the cut again but could not face that same journey in reverse. Regardless of expense he flew back to Marseilles, via Rome, to retrieve his car and continue the gipsy life of a tournament professional.

A sad lapse from grace

In the entire world of professional golf it would be difficult to find a player whose behaviour is as exemplary as that of Mark McNulty. The dapper South African manages to play golf at the highest level without ever putting a toe across the line which distinguishes the perfect gentleman.

He meets his share of frustrations and tribulations with unruffled equanimity. No unseemly word has ever passed his lips in response to an outrageous rub of the green. No one has ever observed him smack a clubhead testily into the turf to release a surge of uncontainable emotion. As for throwing a club, the very idea is absurd in relation to McNulty. Of course he suffers the torture which this thumbscrew of a game imposes on its adherents, but when he bleeds it is an internal haemorrhage behind a mask of bland unconcern.

This steely self-control is matched by a winning personality. He is invariably polite and respectful, considerate and modest. He does not have to work at it; it comes naturally to him. Every pro is happy to be drawn to play with McNulty because it is a guarantee of a tranquil round.

When he plays in Japan he is sensitive to the reverential ambience which surrounds the game of golf and he is one of the few foreign players who lives up to Japanese expectations of a tournament pro as the high priest of a sacred cult.

The purpose of this paean is not to promote McNulty's candidature for canonization but to provide essential background briefing for full appreciation of the exquisite embarrassment which he suffered during the third round of the Japanese Open of 1979.

A few more words are probably necessary to set the scene. It is customary for Japanese spectators to find a promising vantage point and then settle there for the day, furnishing themselves with all the creature comforts required to sustain them during their lengthy vigil.

McNulty was two strokes off the lead when he played an excellent approach shot to a green set in a semi-circle of crowded grandstands. The ball finished five feet above the hole, to the delight of the gallery, and McNulty had a very good chance to press his challenge if he could hole this delicate birdie putt. It would need the most sensitive touch and McNulty judged that the roll of the ball would swing in about two inches from the right. He set himself to this task with every nerve in his body tuned to the problem of delivering the clubface with the touch of a surgeon's scalpel along the precise vector which would deliver the ball surely into the cup.

As he took the club back his concentration was shattered by the crash of a spiked golf shoe descending heavily onto the grandstand steps. McNulty stood away from the ball, his face expressionless. He observed the culprit, an elderly man heavily encumbered with baskets and packages who was attempting to mount to a seat. His innocent ambition was temporarily suspended because, in the face of a massed hissing sound from the other spectators, he stood absolutely frozen, with one foot poised in mid-air above the next step.

Silence was restored and McNulty returned to his putt. The fatigue factor in the human calf muscle of a heavily laden man of advanced years is, as was now demonstrated, a few milliseconds shorter than the time it takes a professional golfer to complete a short putt.

Another crash from the grandstand interrupted McNulty on the backswing. He stood aside from the ball, revealing by not so much as the flicker of an eyelid any trace of emotion. The crowd hushed and shushed and the embarrassed cause of the commotion scrambled up the steps to the stable platform of the first landing stage, where he stood like a statue.

McNulty waited until the simmering crowd settled into respectful silence and started his routine again. In fiction it would be overstraining credulity to contrive yet another disturbance, but life makes its own rules. The heavy-footed spectator had clearly decided that his best course of action was to wait until McNulty putted and then make a dash for his seat, so that he would be safely settled before the next golfer was ready to play. He was therefore, both mentally and physically, in the position of a sprinter poised in his blocks for the gun. Like many a sprinter before him he beat the gun. His footfall echoed round the amphitheatre like a clap of thunder, with the lightning sear-

ing through McNulty's body. His delicate stroke was transformed into a convulsive spasm and the ball missed the hole by a clear five inches, rolling a good four feet past.

McNulty walked slowly across the green and spoke in even tones to one of his Japanese playing companions. 'Would you be so kind as to ask the crowd to settle down comfortably so that I may be assured of playing my next putt without interruption.' The player duly addressed the grandstand and his words were greeted with a murmur of heartfelt sympathy. The old man was safely seated, his face magenta with embarrassment.

Not a muscle twitched among the multitude as McNulty lined up the putt, set himself to the ball and took the club back.

At that moment the old man dropped his lunch basket.

It was not the leaden thump which would be occasioned by the dropping of your average British Open Championship cheese-and-tomato sandwich. It was not the splodge made by the impact of the all-American hamburger with its soggy garnish of mustard, ketchup and relish. It was the cataclysm of a carefully planned and lovingly prepared Japanese picnic lunch, with numerous delicacies and accompanying sauces, each in individual porcelain dishes. It was the shattering of a bamboo container for the boiled rice. It was the explosion of a glass container of nourishing fluid. It was the sundering of chopsticks. It was twenty different explosions, each with its individual pitch and tone close to the pain barrier of the human ear.

McNulty's putt missed the hole by a generous margin. He felt empty and numb. He tapped the ball into the hole, retrieved it and lobbed it in a gentle parabola to his caddie. Nothing snapped inside him, the way it is supposed to snap among men *in extremis*. Nevertheless he felt himself drawn beyond the limit of human endurance. The spirit can take so much and unless he could give vent to the intolerable pressure of his anguish he felt he must surely explode. McNulty grasped his putter in both hands, raised it shoulder high and brought it down, simultaneously raising his right knee.

It was his intention merely to mime the action of man in the grip of uncontrollable anger. He would stop the downward travel of the club a millimetre from his thigh. His torment would be released and the crowd would laugh, dissipating its collective guilt, and everyone would be back to normal.

That was the theory. However, the workings of the central nervous system are impaired by extremes of emotion and McNulty's intentions were betrayed by his reflexes. To his horror he felt the shaft of the putter make contact with his thigh muscles. He looked at the club and saw that it resembled a perfect right angle. He clamped his hand over the shameful elbow which the shaft had acquired and pressed hard with his thumb, hoping to straighten the steel tubing before the crowd could comprehend what he had done.

The medical term, I believe, is crepitus. It describes the grinding together of the sundered elements of a broken bone. In the palm of his hand McNulty detected crepitus as the shaft separated into two parts. At least he was able to complete his plan. He held the putter aloft, his hand firmly hiding the fracture, and the crowd laughed and cheered. What a man. What control. How engaging to feign anger when genuine fury would have been more than warranted. Here was the ultimate expression of the golfing priesthood.

McNulty felt diminished and miserable. As a golfer he was destroyed for this tournament. He putted with his driver and his one-iron for a round of 77.

Some days you just can't fight it

George Burns rightly prides himself on being a good professional, a man with the strength of golf and character to get round a course in respectable figures no matter how bad the conditions. He was not therefore unduly perturbed when a cold wind sprang up for the last round of the Tournament Players' Championship of 1979 at Sawgrass. The US Tour players were accustomed to a bit of rough treatment from the elements in the Florida springtime. After three rounds Burns lay only three strokes behind Lanny Wadkins, the leader, and as he felt the keen wind on his face that Sunday morning Burns judged it to be a 73 or 74 kind of day. A score in that region might not be good enough to win but it ought to be within the capabilities of a solid tournament professional. Most players make that kind of assessment before they go out to play; it keeps them on an even emotional keel if things do not go too well over the early holes.

On the first tee Burns had an eerie feeling: he did not know how to play golf. This is absurd, he told himself, of course I know how to play golf. Dammit, I've been a successful tournament player for four years, not to mention a solid grounding as an amateur. Nevertheless, shuffle as he might, he could not set himself into a position from which to make a pass at the ball. He felt helpless, desperate even. But there was nothing he could do. The starter had called his name, his playing companions were waiting. He had to make a swing. Somehow the clubhead made contact with the ball but the shot was far from impressive.

And so it continued. He tried every adjustment he could think of, without avail. 'I felt my swing was just swirling in the air,' he said afterwards. Burns felt impotent and frustrated and it is at such moments of sinking morale that golfers recall examples of players losing their form totally overnight.

That had happened to Peter Mills, the British Ryder Cup golfer for whom a glittering future had been predicted. Mills had to drop out of golf entirely and eventually regained his amateur status. Burns went round in 83 listless and more or less accidental strokes and was shattered. It was the worst day of his life, the first time he had ever seriously considered walking off a golf course in mid-round. It was not so much the score as the manner of his play that gave Burns nightmares for the next few days. The following week Burns scored a 67 in the first round of the Heritage Classic and the crisis was over. Besides, in golf the one certainty is that you can always take comfort from somebody else's worse disaster. On that horrendous day Bob Murphy scored 92.

An air club

Joe Hagler was getting close to the point where frustration merges into despair. He was four over par in the qualifying round for the Hawaiian Open and needed to make things happen if he was to have any chance at all of getting into the tournament. If golfers were fitted with safety valves, like pressure cookers, his would have been emitting whistling noises and puffs of steam as he snatched his putter from the bag. In the violence of this action his hand caught the skirt of the head cover on his driver and projected the club high into the air, twisting and somersaulting in the manner of a trampolinist performing a complex routine.

Hagler and his caddie, Big Brian, both made reflex grabs at the empty air in the way that children leap in dismay when they let go of gas-filled balloons. The club, as you have surely guessed, landed plumb on Hagler's ball. Indeed, it landed with such precision that the ball did not change position except for being pressed slightly into the turf. That curious circumstance offered a ray of hope to the desperate Hagler. He threw himself on the mercy of the rules official, arguing that Rule 27-1d specified that a penalty was incurred only when a ball was accidentally *moved* by a player's equipment. He even contemplated seeking a free drop for a ball embedded on the fairway but decided not to press his luck. The official declined to share Hagler's optimistic definition of movement and the player had a week's enforced vacation.

Double Dutch

The Dutch Open Championship of 1978 forces its way into any anthology of golf disasters through sheer novelty. Player-power has often been exercised to sort out injustices and absurdities at golf tournaments but this was the only occasion when a major tournament was seriously disrupted by a sit-down strike.

The genesis of the dispute was an agreement between the European Golf Association and what was then the European Tournament Players' Division of the PGA. Because of the increasing number of young American players who were coming to Europe, to gain experience while waiting to gain cards to compete on the US Tour, it had been agreed that all competitors on the European circuit must be members of a recognized professional golfers' association. The Dutch Golf Federation was a party to that agreement which, as soon transpired, was so loosely worded that it was capable of different interpretations.

The Dutch officials, for example, believed that there were no restrictions on the ten invitations allocated to the sponsor. These invitations, they subsequently argued, were in their gift and they could offer them to anyone they liked. Accordingly, they extended invitations to Scott Simpson, Bobby Risch and Kurt Cox, none of whom had won an American card. They were not, therefore, eligible for membership of the American PGA.

The players, acting through the tournament committee,

claimed that these three golfers were not eligible to play in the Dutch Open, either as qualifiers or as invitees.

The argument raged in private meetings all through a long day on the eve of the championship at Noordwijk. Tony Gray, the PGA's tournament director, moved from meeting to meeting seeking to reconcile the opposing factions.

The Dutch refused to withdraw the invitations. The three players declined to withdraw voluntarily. Both sides dug in their heels, despite Gray's calm diplomacy. The Dutch insisted that the championship would proceed as planned. So it did, with a field of 25 Dutch players, who were not party to the dispute, and the three Americans.

Throughout that farcical day's play more meetings were held. Gradually commonsense began to prevail, if such a term can be applied to the processes which produced a compromise of Alice in Wonderland dimensions.

The first round would be eliminated. Officially it had not taken place, although cash rewards would be paid from a separate fund. The championship would be reduced to three rounds and the Americans would be allowed to play, although their results would not count in the championship. They would be paid according to their results in the championship but the cash would come from another separate fund.

And so off they went, with the field containing three phantom players who were both competing and not competing. The compromise offered the bizarre prospect that if, say, Scott Simpson had the lowest total he would receive the equivalent of the first prize but the runner-up would get the official first prize, and the trophy and the title.

Fate missed out on that delicious opportunity but there was a certain irony in the result. The winner was Bob Byman, who 12 months earlier had been in precisely the same situation as his three compatriots. Luckily, by this time he had qualified for membership of the ETPD.

7

Whose side are you on?

Our antagonist is our helper
Edmund Burke

Chinks in the Iron Curtain

To listen to the players you might get the impression that caddies are walking disasters. That is a very narrow and prejudiced view. It is not difficult to cite golfers who could not have become successful players without the guidance of their caddies, and in these days of mechanical golf the caddie carries a heavy responsibility for measuring the course and largely supplying the judgement from which the player selects his club.

In many cases the caddie also performs a valuable passive role as a convenient scapegoat. When a player mishits a shot it is excellent therapy for him to be able to turn on the caddie and berate him roundly for some imaginary malfeasance, misfeasance or nonfeasance. That is accepted by the caddies as all part of the job although, occasionally, this function of being used as a receptacle for vented spleen becomes too much to bear. On one memorable occasion at Wentworth the Professor laid down Ken Brown's bag and gave the golfer a stern lecture on the unprofessional practice of throwing in the towel. 'The one thing I cannot stand,' said the Professor, 'is a quitter.' Whereupon he quit and walked back to the clubhouse.

The travelling caddies who regularly follow the European circuit must of necessity be men of deep resource, for they have to cover vast distances between jobs and, since they rarely get expenses of any kind and are paid at a modest enough rate, they must perforce on occasion substitute ingenuity for rail and air fares. It is just as well that caddies submerge their real identities in nicknames for that prudent safeguard enables me to relate how Irish John solved the problem of getting from Dublin to Berlin for the 1980 German Open Championship even though he did not have two pennies to bless himself with at the time.

Actually it is presumptuous of me to claim that I will relate how he did it, for the stratagems involved in evading ticket collectors are carefully guarded secrets. It must suffice for me to pass on the intelligence that 'Ferries is easy.' As for trains, 'There's ways.' Thus Irish John was able to join up with ten other caddies on the boat train to the continent and it did not present much of a problem at this stage of the journey that, because of Irish John's informal travelling arrangements, the eleven caddies could muster only ten passports between them. However, since Berlin is an enclave of freedom deep behind the Iron Curtain, the party had to pass the close scrutiny of the East German border guards and immigration authorities, not to mention the railway officials and the *Volkspolizei*, the dreaded vopos with itchy trigger-fingers.

Irish John was swathed in coats and deposited on the luggage rack, with cases piled on top of him, and successfully evaded detection although there was one alarming moment involving an innocent French passenger when the stowaway noisily broke wind. On arrival in Berlin Irish John brazenly upbraided an official for not having given him a visa, protesting indignantly that he had been in the toilet when they were issued. He got both a visa and an apology and the first, and easiest, part of the trip was successfully completed. Getting out of Berlin is quite a different matter. It is now that the full weight of East German bureaucracy is brought to bear on the departing traveller in order to thwart escapes to the West.

The caddies obtained permission to ride in the mobile tournament office, a converted truck of uncertain age and disposition under the command of a French driver who spoke no word of English.

They piled the golf bags of their masters into this ancient camion, having first removed the heavy canvas travelling covers. They zipped themselves into these covers and lay on the floor of the camion like so many pupating butterflies in their cocoons. At checkpoint Baker they feigned sleep when the armed guards inspected the camion. Now, according to their pre-arranged plan, they one by one unzipped their cases and emerged, one of their number bearing a bundle of ten passports. Naturally the officials wanted to match each passport against its owner and this proved to be a frustrating task for as each caddie was checked and passed for exit he zipped himself back into his golf bag cover and lay down. Among the squirming mass of pupae it was possible to lose Irish John in the shuffle, although a suspicious official did notice that one of the covers had not extruded a mad caddie. He imperiously undid the zipper, only to reveal the bag and clubs of Sandy Lyle.

The camion was eventually permitted to make its creaking departure through the checkpoint and onto the autobahn leading to Bavaria. It is, of course, strictly *verboten* for traffic in transit to leave the autobahn and it is virtually impossible to turn off it inadvertently. The caddies settled to their slumbers and were awakened by the unaccustomed motion of the camion negotiating sharp corners. The French driver had accidentally left the autobahn and was travelling slowly and illegally through the East German countryside

Roared obscenities were totally lost on him. So was everything else. He knew that he must seek directions and pulled into, of all places, the yard of a police station.

The luck which had attended the caddies did not desert them. An extremely cooperative policeman got into his car and led the camion right back to the slip road onto the autobahn. The caddies were still shouting '*Danke*' as the French driver pulled onto the autobahn – in the wrong direction. They were headed back to Berlin.

This time the chorus of foul abuse had its effect. The driver shrugged his comprehension and made a U-turn across the central reservation, right in front of an autobahn police car. Eventually the policeman tired of roaring abuse and threats at this motley party, none of whom understood a word of his tirade, and let them go on their way.

Apart from taking two days, and having to stop and tie the carburettor into position with a length of fence wire, the rest of the journey to the Swiss Open Championship was uneventful.

Parting is such sweet sorrow

Horace Hutchinson, the most literate of the early golf chroniclers, did not conceal his contempt for caddies. He advised that it was unkind to reward these feckless vagabonds too liberally because they would only over-indulge in strong drink, to the detriment of their health and distress of their families.

In the raggle-taggle fraternity of travelling caddies there are still social misfits and human derelicts, but the majority of caddies are hard-working professionals who make a valuable contribution to the success of their employers.

That is not to say that there are no eccentrics or colourful characters left among the bag-carriers. One such is Chingy, a cheery Cockney whose toothless grin and lurid vocabulary were for years the grace notes to the sombre fugue of Neil Coles's golf.

Eventually Chingy's feet wore out. Out of loyalty Coles kept him in work although the hobbling Chingy found it increasingly difficult to keep up with the play. Chingy's feet precipitated the final crisis during a practice round before the 1972 Open Championship at Muirfield.

This being Scotland there were enormous crowds and Coles was becoming increasingly embarrassed at having to keep urging Chingy to raise his pace. Finally, on the 18th fairway, with thousands watching from the grandstands, and, more to the point, listening, Coles spoke quietly to Chingy: 'Listen, old friend, the championship starts tomorrow and we can't go on like this. It's not fair on you. How about if I pay you for a week's work but get somebody else. . . .'

He never had a chance to complete the question. Chingy released the handle of the trolley with a dramatic gesture which suggested that it was electrified.

At the top of his voice he roared: 'You ******* ****!' He turned with all the dignity available to an old man in a shabby raincoat and rubber boots and took a few painful steps towards the gallery ropes. He then stopped and shouted: 'Colesie! You are a chicken ****!' He took a few more paces and turned again. 'You've always been a chicken ******* ****.' With the linguistic facility which all Cockneys command, he then worked an adjectival variation into his rhetoric. 'And you always ******* will be a ******* chicken ****!'

He had almost reached the side of the fairway when he stopped once more and retraced his steps. Coles stood his ground, transfixed with embarrassment and braced for the next broadside. Chingy reached into the nether recesses of his voluminous clothing and, to a mighty cheer from the spectators, hurled something at close range at his former master. 'And here's your ******* car keys!'

Morocco-bound

The Moroccan Grand Prix for the handsome trophy in the form of a bejewelled dagger, awarded by King Hassan II, is as much a social event as a golf tournament, with much dinner-jacketed feasting at royal palaces, not that this side of things concerns the caddies.

For the most part the professionals and their amateur partners employ the regular caddies of the Royal Dar-es-Salaam club, but some players greatly prefer to use the men who work for them week after week. Mind you, this preference does not always extend to the offer of travelling expenses. The arrangement in many cases is: 'If you can get yourself to the tournament then you can have the job.'

Since Morocco is an out of season event, most of the itinerant professional caddies had gone to Spain for the winter of 1979 in search of rich pickings from holidaymakers on the Costa del Sol. Four of them were in Marbella when loyalty and the lure of fat percentage bonuses decided them to travel to Morocco. One of them took the precaution of telephoning the Moroccan Embassy to inquire whether work permits would be needed and he was reassured that this was not the case.

The four of them loaded up a car and set off on the fairly complicated journey from Algeciras, across the Mediterranean by ferry to Tangier, and then through the most hazardous section of the trip, the perilous negotiation of the customs and immigration departments.

Along the way, in the haphazard style which seems to rule the ad hoc arrangements of travelling caddies, they came across another of their number, Freaky John, squatting by the roadside.

He too squeezed into the car and they arrived at Rabat just in time for the first round. Dave and Pete indeed had to go straight out onto the course.

Very shortly a member of the Royal Moroccan Golf Federation caught up with them and explained politely that he was sorry but only Moroccan caddies were permitted to work during the tournament that year. This edict had come from the Minister of Labour himself.

Hell hath no fury like that of a professional caddie who has spent two days in a rickety car, using his own money, to get to a tournament and then finds that he has no prospect of turning an honest penny. In any rating of citizens whose demeanour equates with the fury which hell cannot match, a tournament professional who is summarily deprived of his favourite caddie probably ranks in second place. And a very close third comes the wealthy amateur who has laid out several thousand bucks, and bribed his club secretary for a phoney handicap certificate, and then sees his vision of silverware receding because his pro is too upset to bring home the birdies and eagles.

Uproar and chaos followed, with professionals and amateurs threatening to pack their bags and depart upon the instant. This venom was directed at officials of the Moroccan Federation who were, of course, powerless to rescind the law of the land and, since the King was President of the Federation, reluctant to flout it. For about two hours the tournament was in the balance until oil was poured upon the turbulent waters. The oil took the form of £50 compensation for each of the foreign caddies who, true to the Bedouin tradition, quietly folded their tents and disappeared into the night.

'The old pro has lost it'

Simon Hobday was getting more and more frustrated during the third round of the 1974 Open Championship at Royal Lytham and St Anne's. Even at the best of times the volcanic Rhodesian engages in fierce verbal warfare with himself on the course, muttering dire insults about his talents and his psychological fitness for golf. This chatter can be unnerving for spectators because Hobday addresses his lurid remarks in the third person and it sounds as if he is talking about someone else. 'The old pro has lost it. He's got the heart of a chicken. What makes the idiot think he can play this game?' I have omitted the adjectives for the sake of brevity.

On this occasion Hobday was suffering on the greens to a degree which would have curdled the soul of a saint. Eleven putts hit the hole and lipped out. After the last of these traumas he followed his normal practice of throwing the putter at his golf bag lying by the side of the green. This time the club landed exactly on the point of balance and, with the shaft vibrating wildly, it rebounded and landed in the semi-rough a few yards away.

His caddie was busy replacing the flagstick at this moment and had not observed the kangaroo antics of the putter. He simply picked up the bag and bore it to the next tee, and on down the subsequent par five to the next green. 'What have you done with the putter?' demanded Hobday. The caddie, fearful that his career was about to be nipped in the bud in a tirade of expletives, declared his innocence of its whereabouts. 'It must be lying by the last green. Nip back and fetch it,' commanded Hobday.

Seeking to retain as much dignity as possible in the turmoil of his confusion the caddie began to march briskly back down the fairway. With a total disregard for the sensibilities of the gallery Hobday shouted: 'Run, you bugger!'

The caddie ran, all the way to the previous green and all the way back again, bearing the truant putter. To his surprise he saw that Hobday had already driven off the next tee and was clearly in good spirits. 'Trust the old pro to improvise in an emergency,' he announced to himself smugly.

The caddie asked what had happened. 'The old pro used his two-iron,' said Hobday, 'and he holed his 25-footer.'

A rosette by any other name

Yes, by all means let us consider the lilies of the field. The clear message is that they do not need gilding. That was the mistake made by the young tournament administrator when he set up the golf course for the Italian Open Championship of 1976. That year the Open was held at Is Molas, a new course in Sardinia. The terrain along the southern coast of this island consists of low, rocky hills and the course was built on alluvial deposits through valleys. In order to deflect flood water from the hills the architect had provided a cement drainage channel down the side of the 16th fairway. In the local rules for the championship it was clearly written that a ball lying in or over the drain was out of bounds. So far so good.

However, the tournament administrator, a man much given to toiling and spinning in the interests of his players, deemed it prudent to reinforce the message by knocking white out-of-bounds stakes into the ground alongside the drain. That was gilding the lily and he further decided to give it two coats of gilt by banging in some red stakes as well. Thus there could be no possible doubt that the construction was indeed the drain in question and that it was out of bounds.

Now anybody who has tried to knock a stake into the ground in southern Sardinia will gladly volunteer the information that the task is easier said that done, since the earth consists of 97 per cent rocks with a meagre bonding of thin soil. Perhaps all would have been well if the stakes had been positioned on the golf course side of the drain. But no, they had to go the other side and what happened was that a stake when banged with a mallet would strike a rock the size of a baby's head and skid sideways six inches or so. In some cases it proved impossible to get the stakes within a yard of the drain. Admittedly, it was a chance in a million but there was now a narrow strip of no-man's-land alongside the drain which was out of bounds according to the local rule but in bounds according to the championship rules in regard to coloured stakes.

Murphy's law came into operation during the final round when the teenaged Sam Torrance was making a run for the championship. His ball came to rest on that sliver of ambiguous territory.

Sam sought guidance from older and wiser heads, including his playing companion, the experienced Billy Casper. Since it was clearly inside the line of white stakes Casper gave it as his opinion that the ball was in play. Torrance was unconvinced. After further discussion he was relieved to see an electric cart bearing down on the scene with three officials. It was driven by a man dressed in the blazer of the Federazione Italiano di Golf and wearing the ornate rosette which distinguished the official referees. He spoke no English but he made it amply clear that the ball was not out of bounds.

Torrance proceeded accordingly, dropping under penalty on the fairway, and a few minutes later he handed in his card. The urbane chief referee spoke to this effect: 'I cannot accept your card, Torrance. You were observed following an incorrect procedure on the 16th fairway, at variance with the local rule, and your score for that hole is incorrect. You are disqualified.'

Torrance was dumbstruck. He ran wildly from the recorder's tent and across the golf course so that his friends would not see the tears which were welling in his eyes. He was distracted with anger and grief and disappointment and shame.

Around the clubhouse there was pandemonium. It transpired that the ruling had indeed been given by a member of the Italian Federation, the acting President Signor S. Antonio Roncoroli, no less, but that he was not an official referee. In law he was just a spectator, an agency outside the game. Incensed senior professionals besieged the committee room. Under a barrage of protest, insult, threat and a whiff of open revolt, officialdom agreed to review the case. Rule 36-5 was considered: 'The Committee has no power to waive a Rule of Golf. A penalty of disqualification, however, may, in exceptional individual cases, be waived or be modified or be imposed if the Committee consider such action warranted.'

In view of the very real likelihood that the members of the committee would be torn limb from limb if they upheld the disqualification decision, they ruled after 3½ hours of discussion that this was an exceptional individual case and the penalty be waived. Torrance went on to finish in a tie for fourth place.

When homicide might be justifiable

The importance of winning tournaments is obvious enough for golfers. A player can make a living on place money but it takes victories to earn a fortune. The victory march is no less important for caddies, even though it may be in a minor financial key. After all, it is quite common for a tournament professional to have a standing agreement with his regular caddie to pay 7 per cent of prize winnings as a bonus on top of the retainer. In these days of five- and six-figure first prizes the caddie's 7 per cent can set him up nicely.

There was a lot of money at stake back in 1960 when Bob Goalby played himself into the comfortable position of having three putts to win the Coral Gables Open in Miami. Goalby was probably the calmest man on the golf course. The crowds were excited and so, naturally enough, was Goalby's 17-year-old caddie. This was his first chance for a jackpot bonus and his main concern was to get the gallery settled and quiet so that his man could putt out in peace. The lad walked to the side of the green, motioning with his hands like a conductor taking the orchestra into a *piano* passage. With his eyes still on the crowd, he moved back to take up position at the flag and as he did so he kicked Goalby's ball right off the green.

Goalby's comfortable position was now critical. As a young player he had a low boiling point and his emotions at this stage were a jumble of explosive impulses, mainly an intense desire to strangle the aghast caddie. This was hardly the frame of mind for a delicate chip shot, and as he settled to the ball his problems were compounded by the distraction of a rhythmic whooshing sound: Dow Finsterwald warming up on the adjacent first tee with practice swings in preparation for the play-off.

He chipped to five feet and then hit a miserable putt, but the ball lurched towards the hole and toppled in on the last gasp. Thus the danger of homicide was averted and Goalby and the caddie enjoyed a long and profitable partnership. It is not much consolation at the time but it is nevertheless a fact that every time a golfer runs into a disaster it is possible to delve back into history and discover an even worse disaster of the same type.

In this case we can cite the case of Byron Nelson who lost the 1946 US Open no less, at Canterbury Country Club, Cleveland, Ohio, when his caddie accidentally kicked his ball on the 16th green in the third round. Nelson was penalized a stroke and finished with a total of 284. A score of 283 would have won the championship but that extra penalty stroke put him into a play-off with Lloyd Mangrum and Mangrum won.

Roger Wethered, the English amateur, also dished his chances of capturing a major championship through inadvertent contact of boot and ball on the green. In his case the wound was self-inflicted for on the 14th green at St Andrews in the third round of the 1921 Open Championship he was so engrossed in studying the line of his putt as he walked backwards from the hole towards his ball that he stepped on it. That stroke was the vital one which enabled Jock Hutchison to tie Wethered's total and Hutchison prevailed in the play-off.

A moving ball story

Rule 26 says that if a player's moving ball be stopped or deflected by himself, his partner or either of their caddies or equipment then he shall lose the hole (in matchplay) or incur a penalty of two strokes (in strokeplay). Students of the laws of golf, as which of us isn't, should note the omission of the word 'accidentally' in the framing of these rules. In the related rules, such as ball stopped or deflected by an opponent, or fellow competitor, the wording specifies that the interference must be accidental. Does this, you may ask, mean that the penalty is the same whether you or your caddie deliberately stop your moving ball or whether it was pure accident? On the face of it that might seem to be the case, but the face of it is misleading. Deliberate interference with your moving ball renders you liable to disqualification, which makes the absence of the word 'accidentally' rather puzzling. It is not, I can assure you, a case of unworldly legislators sitting in ivory towers and refusing to countenance the possibility that the player of a gentleman's game would ever stoop to cheating. The Rules of Golf are framed on the assumption that everyone who takes a club in hand, will, given the minutest loophole in the laws, cheat like mad. That is one reason why golfers do not cheat, because every imaginable opportunity for dirty work has been specifically blocked by the lawmakers. The other reason, of course, is that surreptitious cheating is so easy that golf without honesty is simply not worth playing.

For these reasons professional golfers in particular are the most law-abiding citizens in sport. In the first place they are conditioned by the nature of the game to stifle any unseemly notions and in the second place they are surrounded by markers, fellow competitors, opponents and referees just waiting to beat them into insensibility with that draconian rule book.

It follows, then, that instances of golfers being penalized for interference with a moving ball are the result of pure mischance, flukes of the fickle finger of fate, sheer bad luck, Kismet. It further follows that such penalties invariably represent travesties of natural justice.

Imagine then the feelings of Leonard Thompson in the 1978 Quad Cities Open when he rolled a putt up to the hole for an eagle. His caddie, squirming with excitement, was indulging in the rather tiresome practice of performing an elaborate panto-mime designed to demonstrate his loyalty by directing the ball into the hole with extravagant gestures and cries of encourage-ment. A tee peg fell from its normal storage area behind the caddie's ear, dropped onto the green directly in the path of the ball and deflected its run. Two-stroke penalty.

Brian Huggett was the hapless victim of Rule 26 in the days when you were penalized if you or your caddie or equipment were accidentally struck by your opponent's ball. (These days there is no penalty; the procedure now consists of polite apologies all round, followed by the option of playing the ball as it lies or replaying the stroke.)

Huggett was seeking to defend his PGA Matchplay Cham-pionship title at Walton Heath in 1969, and in his semi-final against Dai Rees he was one up with one to play. Rees's do-or-die drive at the last hole went horribly wrong. The ball was hooked wildly and carried only 150 yards before hitting a post carrying the gallery-control ropes. The ball rebounded towards the tee and hit Huggett's golf bag, which his caddie had carried forward into a position which had seemed to be well clear of any danger. Huggett forfeited the hole and was in no emotional state to match Rees's safe par at the first extra hole.

PETER DOBEREINER

Peter Dobereiner is inarguably the most widely traveled golf writer of the day, and arguably the most graceful, the funniest and the most iconoclastic of a generally raffish but uniquely literate breed.

When he's not following professional golf around the world, Dobereiner lives in a rambling house in Kent, England. He has written numerous books on golf, including *The World of Golf* (1981) and *Down the 19th Fairway* (1983), and reckons his output on the game is equivalent to two Bibles. Well-known to American readers through his column in *Golf Digest* magazine, Dobereiner also writes regularly for the London *Observer*.